Cambridge Elements

Elements in Development Economics
Series Editor-in-Chief
Kunal Sen
UNU-WIDER and University of Manchester

DEVELOPMENTAL DILEMMAS

The Role of Power and Agency

William D. Ferguson
Grinnell College

CAMBRIDGE
UNIVERSITY PRESS

Shaftesbury Road, Cambridge CB2 8EA, United Kingdom

One Liberty Plaza, 20th Floor, New York, NY 10006, USA

477 Williamstown Road, Port Melbourne, VIC 3207, Australia

314–321, 3rd Floor, Plot 3, Splendor Forum, Jasola District Centre,
New Delhi – 110025, India

Cambridge University Press is part of Cambridge University Press & Assessment,
a department of the University of Cambridge.

We share the University's mission to contribute to society through the pursuit of
education, learning and research at the highest international levels of excellence.

www.cambridge.org
Information on this title: www.cambridge.org/9781009469685
DOI: 10.1017/9781009469647

© UNU-WIDER 2026

This publication is in copyright. Subject to statutory exception and to the provisions of relevant collective licensing agreements, with the exception of the Creative Commons version the link for which is provided below, no reproduction of any part may take place without the written permission of Cambridge University Press & Assessment.

An online version of this work is published at doi.org/10.1017/9781009469647 under a Creative Commons Open Access license CC-BY-NC-SA 3.0 IGO which permits re-use, distribution and reproduction in any medium for non-commercial purposes providing appropriate credit to the original work is given, any changes made are indicated, and the new work is published under the same licence terms. When the licensor is an intergovernmental organisation, disputes will be resolved by mediation and arbitration where possible. To view a copy of this license,
visit https://creativecommons.org/licenses/by-nc-sa/3.0/igo

When citing this work, please include a reference to the DOI 10.1017/9781009469647

First published 2026

A catalogue record for this publication is available from the British Library

A Cataloging-in-Publication data record for this Element is available from the Library of Congress

ISBN 978-1-009-46968-5 Hardback
ISBN 978-1-009-46963-0 Paperback
ISSN 2755-1601 (online)
ISSN 2755-1598 (print)

Additional resources for this publication at www.cambridge.org/ferguson

Cambridge University Press & Assessment has no responsibility for the persistence or accuracy of URLs for external or third-party internet websites referred to in this publication and does not guarantee that any content on such websites is, or will remain, accurate or appropriate.

For EU product safety concerns, contact us at Calle de José Abascal, 56, 1°, 28003 Madrid, Spain, or email eugpsr@cambridge.org

Developmental Dilemmas

The Role of Power and Agency

Elements in Development Economics

DOI: 10.1017/9781009469647
First published online: February 2026

William D. Ferguson
Grinnell College
Author for correspondence: William D. Ferguson, Ferguso1@grinnell.edu

Abstract: Why do well-meaning developmental policies fail? Power intervenes. Consider the recent collapse of the peace agreement between the Colombian government and FARC guerillas. Achieving inclusive development entails resolving collective-action problems of forging cooperation among agents with disparate interests and understandings. Resolution relies on developing functional informal and formal institutions. Powerful agents shape institutional evolution—because they can. This Element outlines a conceptual framework for policy-relevant inquiry. It addresses the concept of power—noting sources, instruments, manifestations, domains of operation, and strategic templates. After discussing leadership, following, and brokerage, it addresses institutional entrepreneurship. Institutional entrepreneurs develop narratives and actions to influence incentives and interpretations of social norms and identities: foundations of strategic interactions that shape institutional evolution. This approach facilitates inquiry into the roots and consequences of context-specific developmental dilemmas: background for developmental policy analysis. This title is also available as open access on Cambridge Core.

Keywords: collective-action problems, triadic power, institutional entrepreneurs, social identities, resource conflict

© UNU-WIDER 2026

ISBNs: 9781009469685 (HB), 9781009469630 (PB), 9781009469647 (OC)
ISSNs: 2755-1601 (online), 2755-1598 (print)

Contents

1 Introduction 1

2 Institutions and Principles of Power 13

3 Foundations of Structural Change: Three Types of Agency 24

4 Institutional Entrepreneurs 44

5 Conflict, Power, Agency, and Developmental Dilemmas 68

References 91

An online appendix for this publication can be accessed at www.cambridge.org/ferguson

1 Introduction

> ... *the enhancement of human freedom is both the main object and primary means of development.*
>
> Amartya Sen, 1999

Why do well-intentioned developmental policies so often fail? Consider the recent collapse of a well-constructed peace agreement between Colombia's government and FARC guerrillas. In Russia, the rapid privatization of Soviet assets fostered authoritarian kleptocracy. Consider the eruption of Hindu-Muslim violence and mass dislocation following the 1947 partition of India from Pakistan – a tragic aftermath of the decades-long struggle for independence from Britain. In Indonesia, transnational palm oil companies adopted socially responsible company policies banning deforestation and observing local rights to free, prior, and informed consent. Yet, implementation failed due to the cooptation of village leaders, secret deals, and intimidation (Afrizal and Berenschot, 2020).

Why such failure? Powerful agents intervene. Others follow.
Functional development entails resolving social dilemmas embedded within myriad collective-action problems. The overarching developmental dilemma concerns how to create a sustainable path to inclusive political and economic development. How might a society establish and nurture broadly distributed political and economic capabilities when powerful agents so often benefit from non-inclusive extractive interactions founded in persistent socially wasteful, exploitative, and repressive relationships? Multiple embedded dilemmas apply. Here are three:

1. *Limiting violence in areas with sharp social cleavages*, such as inter-ethnic acrimony, when powerful actors benefit from continued conflict. A common dilemma in transitional times. Consider the post-1990 emergence of civil war in the former Yugoslavia. President Marshall Tito, who died in 1980, had successfully suppressed ethnic rivalry between Serbs, Croats, Bosniaks, and ethnic Albanians.[1] Subsequently, with prompting by opportunistic regional leaders – notably Slobodan Milosevic in Serbia and Franjo Tudjman in Croatia – inter-ethnic violence emerged and escalated into civil war. Reflecting the conformity-inducing influence of such charismatic divisive leaders, a young Croatian man offered the following comment on his choice between violence and ostracization by his community: "I really don't hate Muslims – but because of the situation I want to kill them all." (Bardhan, 2005, 187, citing Block, 1993, 10.) How then might multiethnic

---

[1] *Bosniaks* are Muslim residents of Bosnia; The *term* Bosnians refers to all residents of Bosnia.

societies encourage ethnic autonomy and recognition without provoking undue social cleavage?
2. *Limiting developmental impasses imposed by systemic corruption* without undermining stability. Competing elites – *patrons* – distribute rents to various *clients*, in return for political support. Political leaders use rents to attain political support and maintain stability (Haber et al., 2003). Such exchanges become an informal foundation of persistent asymmetric power relationships that spawn entrenched reliance on short-term distributions of benefits – rather than investments in long-term development (Khan, 2010; Bebbington et al. 2018; Bardhan and Mookerjee, 2018). Furthermore, patronage-based distributions often underlie relative social peace by coopting potential adversaries. For example, in 1870–1910 Mexico, the corrupt Diaz dictatorship ended decades of civil violence that followed Mexico's struggle for independence from Spain, achieved in 1821. Similarly, after 1920, the systemic corruption of Mexico's dominant Institutional Revolutionary Party (the PRI) largely quelled the decade-long violence of the Mexican Revolution (la Guerra Civil Mexicana).

Moreover, after studying 18 "*pockets of effectiveness*" in five countries, Hickey and Sen (2024, 4) state: "organizational effectiveness required a mix of political loyalty and bureaucratic competence rather than the displacement of patronage by pure forms of meritocracy." Often, the social provision of benefits relies on patron-client politics as well as formal democracy (Carbone, 2009).

A related dilemma: How to achieve political-economic liberalization without fostering oligarchy and corruption. Divesting state assets creates uncertainty regarding their value. Transfers of wealth to oligarchs often follow, as in Russia. Liberalizing product markets often enhances the value of land and natural resources, opening opportunities for capturing rents. Practicing *competitive populism*, political elites can distribute private or club goods in return for support. In "India – corruption is perceived to have gone up in recent post-reform decades." (Bardhan, 2018, 116).
3. Managing contestable resources to achieve stable, inclusive, and productive utilization. Point-source resources, such as gold, minerals, and oil, or lucrative exportable agricultural commodities, such as sugar, cotton, tobacco, and opioids, often facilitate a *resource curse*. Domestic and transnational producers extract rents, dominate politics via clientelist distributions, and truncate economic development. The presence of subsoil resources "defines the terrain on which settlements are constituted, negotiated, and contested." (Bebbington 223). Developmental challenges include diversifying the

economy, fostering long-term investment, structural transformation, and achieving a more equitable distribution.[2]

For over a century, Zambia's copper-belt elites have dominated politics. The population has not shared the benefits of this extensive resource. Moreover, few alternative sources of income exist in industry, and the agricultural sector lacks dynamism. Fluctuations in international copper prices have compounded developmental obstacles. (Levy 2013; Bebbington et al., 2018).

Peru's endowments of oil, copper, silver, zinc, lead, and gold – over 50 percent of its exports – have facilitated a more limited resource curse. Export dependence has left Peru vulnerable to transnational political influence and international price fluctuations. Between 1968 and 1980, attempting to unwind such dependence, Peru's left-wing military government nationalized mines and pursued agrarian reform. Violence, hyperinflation, and isolation from the global financial system undermined the regime. The locus of foreign influence shifted from US mining companies to international creditors (Bebbington et al., 2018). Yet, after 1990, government technocrats reduced inflation and foreign debt. Between 2004 and 2014, annual GDP grew at 6.4 percent, and the government distributed benefits. Poverty fell from 60 percent to 33 percent. After 2014, however, annual growth slowed to 2.3 percent, due to "institutional deterioration, a less favorable external economic context …, the effects of COVID-19, and marked political instability since 2018" (World Bank).[3]

A *resource curse*, however, is not inevitable. In negotiations with international oil firms, Uganda insisted that extracted oil first go to domestic refineries rather than immediate export. Uganda achieved 38–50 percent share of oil profits and insulated oil technocrats from political influence (Hickey and Sen, 2024).

Dilemmas 1–3 often work in tandem. In the Democratic Republic of Congo (DRC; formerly Zaire), extensive mining and oil resources presented a "curse" infused with deep corruption and intense ethnic violence. The conflict involves the government, rebels, and troops sponsored by Rwanda.[4]

How then might developing countries limit disruptive, often violent, social cleavage, unravel systemic corruption, and curb the political influence of extractive elites? How might they achieve inclusive distribution with productive

---

[2] Structural transformation connotes shifting production from agriculture to manufacturing and services, moving from low skill and low-productivity activities to higher skill and higher productivity activities and sectors (Sen, 2023).
[3] www.worldbank.org/en/country/peru/overview.
[4] www.nytimes.com/2025/01/23/world/africa/rwanda-rebels-congo.html?searchResultPosition=1

utilization of mineral and human resources that support broader investment and structural transformation?

Alas, achieving inclusive development entails resolving complex collective-action problems of forging cooperation among agents with disparate interests, capabilities, norms, identities, and policy ideas. Resolution, moreover, depends on functional configurations of informal and formal institutions, with supportive constituencies. Yet, powerful actors, pursuing their own political-economic agendas, shape institutional evolution in their favor – because they can. Distributions of power thus shape the emergence and functioning of institutions and, by extension, developmental trajectories that condition prospects for functional policy and reform.

A systematic approach to power theory, as it relates to agency, collective action, and institutional evolution thus offers a lens for critical inquiry into the roots and consequences of developmental dilemmas, as well as a theoretical foundation for policy analysis. Accordingly, this Element outlines a conceptual framework for analyzing how developmental dilemmas that emerge from context-specific distributions of power, malleable understandings, and associated CAPs undermine prospects for inclusive development. Functional development policy depends on understanding these principles.

Readers may approach this text from several angles. Those less interested in mathematical representation can grasp the principles without focusing on models and equations. Those more interested in modeling can find more detailed, yet approachable, game-theoretic models in several on-line appendices. Intended audiences include advanced undergraduates in economics and political science; graduate students in applied masters, master's, MSc, or Ph.D. programs related to political economy, development, and policy analysis. Postdoctoral researchers, policy analysts at think tanks, NGOs, and government agencies, and established scholars in these fields may also find my systematic integrative approach useful.

1.1 Related Literature

Existing development and political economy literature points to important relationships and mechanisms, but it often fails to offer sufficiently comprehensive analysis. For example, the principal-agent literature addresses implications of asymmetric information, yielding insight into economic and political interactions, including labor-management, supplier-producer, and citizen-government. Even so, it focuses too narrowly on bilateral relationships and abstracts from the varied influences of social norms, group identities, and complex power relationships involving third parties.

In contrast, this Element synthesizes diverse components of often-separate literatures. It builds on overlapping approaches to the political economy of power, institutions, and development that appear in six related literatures:

1. *Collective Action Theory*: Following paths developed by Mancur Olson (1965) and Elinor Ostrom (1990), this Element poses collective-action problems as a critical obstacle to functional development. "What is missing from the policy analyst's tool kit – and from the set of accepted, well-developed theories of human organization – is an adequately specified theory of collective action whereby a group of principals can organize themselves voluntarily to retain the residuals of their own effort" (Ostrom, 1990, 22).
2. *New institutionalism* (e.g., North, 1990; Greif, 2006; Acemoglu and Robinson, 2012): a rational-choice approach, with a historical perspective, that addresses institutions as "the rules of the game in society." Institutions shape incentives, preferences, information flows, and common understandings of social environments. The underappreciated and too often ignored cognitive thread of institutional influence implies an interactive connection between incentives and shared understandings – or, equivalently, interests and ideas. Configurations of informal and formal institutions thus condition interactions among individuals and organizations and so underlie developmental obstacles and potential.
3. *The foundational role of informal institutions* (e.g., Elster, 1989; North, 1990; Basu, 2000). Social norms constitute important elements of social equilibria that mediate the effectiveness and functionality of formal institutions and policies. Laws and formal rules that do not point to social equilibria are not institutions; they are just words on paper (Basu, 2000).
4. *Social conflict theory of institutions* (Knight, 1992; Bowles, 2004; Acemoglu and Robinson, 2005; Hall and Thelen, 2009; Mahoney and Thelen, 2009; Tilly and Tarrow, 2015). Incorporating both history and current interactions, this approach posits an *ecology of conflict* among distinct strategic agents. Organizations and individuals employ coordinated efforts to advance distinct claims that affect others' interests. Underlying beliefs and distributions of power shape the emergence and demise of powerful coalitions that influence institutional trajectories. Agents test the limits of cooperative agreements and processes of mobilization that bring other actors in line with those agreements' (Hall and Thelen, 2009, 13). Institutions thus "represent relatively durable yet continuously contested settlements based on specific coalitional dynamics" (Mahoney and Thelen, 2009, 8). Within such dynamics, the impetus for institutional innovation

arises from grievances over distribution and participation. Methods of innovation, however, evolve from reinforcing adaptive feedback as rules and patterns become increasingly established. At given points in time, institutional configurations emerge from pre-games. *Pre-games* establish rules of subsequent games, which then condition interactions and ensuing political-economic outcomes (Aoki, 2001). Institutions thus arise and operate as both outcomes of power relations and as sources of power that shape incentives, understandings, behavior, and political-economic development.

5. Political settlement analysis (PSA: e.g., Di John and Putzel, 2009; Khan, 2010; Kelsall et al., 2022). PSA extends and formalizes institutional conflict theory. This approach facilitates analyzing the foundational role of distributions of power in shaping the emergence and operation of institutions, with corresponding impact on distribution, information flows, agents' motivations, and understandings of social context. A political settlement is "an ongoing agreement among a society's most powerful groups over a set of political and economic institutions expected to generate for them a minimally acceptable level of benefits, which thereby ends or prevents generalized civil war and/or political and economic disorder" (Kelsall et al., 2022). In this approach, a typology of settlements combines two spectra:[5]

   i. The *social foundation*, meaning the groups that possess sufficient disruptive power to merit inclusion in the settlement: insiders. The social foundation ranges from relatively broad (many groups) to narrow (a few exclusive groups).
   ii. The *configuration of power* among insiders ranges from coherent (or unipolar) to incoherent (or multipolar). A coherent configuration of power implies resolution of basic organizational CAPs regarding how to allocate authority, with corresponding (rough) agreement on major issues, such as relationships between the state and the market or the state and religion. An incoherent configuration implies no such coherence, with a corresponding need to continuously renegotiate initiatives and policies.

Each of the typology's four quadrants implies distinct types of developmental dilemmas with distinct prospects for resolving collective-action problems of establishing and maintaining functional institutions. Moreover, to persist, a settlement's institutional configurations must deliver sufficient rents to powerful insiders – enough to deter using their power to overturn the settlement. Discretionary allocation of rents is the currency of politics (Levy, 2014).

---

[5] Kelsall and vom Hau (2019) developed the initial version of this typology. Ferguson (2020) uses slightly different terminology for the *configuration of power* axis: the *configuration of authority*, which ranges from *unipolar* to *multipolar*.

Punctuated-equilibrium dynamics follow. PSA offers a largely macro-level lens for context-specific developmental analysis. Appendix I elaborates.[6]

6. *Interests, Ideas, and political entrepreneurs* (Mukand and Rodrik, 2018; Ash et al., 2024): This supply-side approach to politics addresses the joint influence of ideas and interests on politics, merging often separately discussed topics. Ideas influence perceptions of interests. Interests provide incentives to acquire, hold, and propagate ideas. Ideas are "hooks on which politicians hang their objectives and further their interests" (Shepsle and Noll, 1985). *Ideational politics* combines ideas and interests, using an evolutionary dynamic. *Political entrepreneurs* introduce memes.[7] *Memes* are narratives, symbols, and actions that operate like evolutionary genes (Dawkins, 1976). Their propagation responds to social selection by voters, interests, and policymakers. Ideas that appear to foster successful outcomes spread. Others fail. There are two types of ideational politics: *Worldview politics* focuses on political-economic understandings of interests. *Identity politics* focuses on norms and concepts of group identity, with corresponding ideas of inclusion and exclusion. Political-economy dynamics thus reflect combined and evolving influences of interests, worldview, and identity politics. Shifting degrees of meme acceptance and rejection signal understandings of interests, obligations, and group identities that condition prospects for cooperation and conflict in political-economic development.

My approach merges and extends perspectives from these six literatures. I incorporate a rational choice/historical take on collective action (#1) with institutions as rules of the game (#2); reflecting the influences of norms on social equilibria (#3); all conditioned by social conflict theory of institutions (#4). I add political settlements analysis (#5) and dynamic feedback between interests and ideational politics (#6). Additionally, utilizing a boundedly rational approach, I incorporate cognitive and behavioral relations between social norms and social identities, along with four specific types of agency: leadership, following, brokerage, and institutional entrepreneurship.[8] I address these relations with a systematic approach to conceptualizing power.

Finally, I incorporate complementary influences from two sets of authors: *Set 1: Daron Acemoglu and James Robinson* (with or without Simon Johnson; hereafter, A &R) offer three pertinent arguments.

---

[6] Related typologies appear in Khan (2010), Levy (2014), and Kelsall and vom Hau (2019).

[7] Ash et al. (2024) note that political entrepreneurship appears in Lenin (1939) and Downs (1957), and was formalized by Bénabou (2008). On identity and politics, they cite Fearon and Laitin (2000).

[8] Bounded rationality implies goal-orientation with limited cognition. Institutional entrepreneurs operate like #6's political entrepreneurs.

1. *Institutions, growth, and power* (AJR, 2005): Institutions structure incentives that underlie long-run growth. Distributions of power, arising from three sources – resource access, institutionally designated positions, and resolved collective-action problems – shape the formation and longevity of political and economic institutions. Ensuing political positions and economic outcomes confer power in the next period, which shapes subsequent trajectories: feedback. Furthermore, absent institutional constraint, powerful actors cannot credibly commit to refraining from using their power for their own future advantage.[9] Thus, functional development entails achieving credible commitments to limit exercises of power – or, as I will elaborate, resolving second-order CAPs.
2. *Extractive vs. Inclusive institutions* (A&R, 2012). This work contrasts the developmental implications of *extractive* – exploitative and hierarchical – institutions as opposed to *inclusive* institutions. Initial conditions, such as resource geography and distributions of power during periods of early colonization, generate critical junctures that indicate two path-dependent longue-durée trajectories:[10]

    i. Narrow elite coalitions establish extractive institutions that truncate development
    ii. Broader coalitions foster (relatively) inclusive institutions and growth.

3. *A narrow pathway to development* (A&R, 2018). This work focuses on the inherent conflict between a *Leviathan* state, which seeks despotic hegemony, and civil society, which seeks to "control and shackle" the state – a collective-action problem. Fruitful development emerges along a "narrow corridor" reflecting a delicate balance of these forces. Herein, competing coalitions make investments in power, with increasing returns, generating three possible steady states:

    I. *Strong society/weak state:* restrictive norms produce a "cage" of informal governance by social elites that inhibits innovation.
    II. *Strong state/weak society*: a despotic state restricts freedom of thought and action, inhibiting economic progress.
    III. *Shackled Leviathan*: Within a *narrow corridor*, civil society limits state power without destroying it, and limited state power curbs "cage" excesses. Liberty and economic growth follow.

I incorporate and revise components of A&R's three arguments. I adopt the 2005 approach to power, institutional evolution, and credibility, but with far

---

[9] Bardhan (2005) makes this point; its origins go back to Hobbes.
[10] Engerman and Sokolof (2002) also relate long-term development to colonial inequality.

greater attention to power's third source: resolution of collective-action problems. I consider their 2012 extractive and inclusive institutions as an opening take on institutional configurations, but I offer more categories and relations, with attention to underlying distributions of power – notably the more nuanced approach of political settlements analysis.

Regarding A&R 2018, I find the *narrow corridor's* delicate balance and role for coalitions instructive. I appreciate their assertion that a normative "cage" restricts opportunity and development – a useful counter to over-glorifying civil society. Nevertheless, as Avanish Dixit recommends, scholars should extend and modify A&R's approach to address "fissures within each of their two players ... and coalitions across subgroups," along with roles for culture, identity, ideology, and non-rational actors (2021, 24). My framework's mix of power, bounded rationality, informal and formal institutions, and social identities – with distinct types of agency – offers a conceptual foundation for addressing Dixit's concerns.

Set 2: Scholars related to the (former) Effective States and Inclusive Development Research Centre of the Global Development Institute at the University of Manchester. These scholars, including Bebbington, Behuria, Hickey, Kelsall, Leftwich, Levy, Pritchett, Schultz, Sen, Werker, Whitfield, and vom Hau, extend the political-settlement approaches of Khan (2010) and Di John and Putzel (2009).[11] Hickey and Sen (2024) summarize and augment these contributions, emphasizing five areas:

- A social configuration of power–that is, the social foundations of political settlements (Kelsall et al., 2022).
- Three sets of ideas: paradigmatic/philosophy; problem definitions; and policy ideas/solutions – noting their normative and cognitive elements.
- Policy domains: how distinct policy problems (e.g., service provision, resource management) operate within different meso-level regions and distributions of power, as well as macro-level interactions between policy domains and political settlements.
- Pockets of effectiveness: domains of local success in regions with substantial developmental dilemmas.
- Ordered deals: informal, yet credible, exchange agreements.

These authors bridge two conceptual gaps:

i. That between a long-durée history based on critical junctures and contemporary institutional configurations. Political settlements tend to persist over

---

[11] Khan (2018) also extends PSA. Behuria (2025) draws a sharp distinction (sharper than I would) between Khan's approach to PSA and approaches related to Kelsall et al.

medium-term time horizons, and they are subject to sometimes dramatic shifts (punctuation of equilibria).
ii. That between macro-and meso-level analysis. Political settlements operate largely at a macro level. Policy domains operate at meso-levels based on regions and policy areas.

I largely utilize their approach, with greater emphasis on detailed power theory, types of agency, collective-action problems, and game-theoretic reasoning, but fewer specifics on policy domains, pockets of effectiveness, and ordered deals.[12]

1.2 Related Debates and My Approach

My integrated approach sheds light on several related debates, without taking a "side." I pursue a middle ground that depends on the social context. A few such debates:

1. The relative roles of the state and market in economic development. They are inextricably linked, even in "liberal" economic settings.
2. The political-economic importance of non-state actors. I highlight roles for unofficial agents who influence the legitimacy of formal institutions and corresponding abilities of formal actors to implement policy.[13]
3. Material interests vs. ideas. They are complementary. Informal and formal institutions establish cognitive frameworks that condition understandings of interests. Institutional entrepreneurs propagate narratives, symbols, and actions that influence understandings of political-economic interests, norms, and social identities. Combinations of ideas and perceived interests motivate strategic responses.
4. Structure and agency: To what degree do institutional structures shape agents' understandings and actions, and to what extent do agents – individuals or organized groups – shape the emergence and evolution of structures? Evolutionary feedback combines both.
5. A "top-down" as opposed to "bottom-up" approach to policy analysis. Both operate simultaneously. Institutional entrepreneurs work at both levels. The feasibility of either depends on social context.[14]

To address these issues, this Element relies on four underlying concepts.

---

[12] Chapter 8 of Ferguson (2020) discusses and models ordered deals.
[13] Lust (2022) emphasizes non-state actors within informal institutional arenas. The public authority literature stresses non-state actors. For a review, see (Kirk and Pennington, 2024).
[14] Matland's (1995) typology relates top-down vs. bottom-up feasibility to policy conflict and ambiguity.

First, following Amartya Sen (2001), I define *development* as the sustainable, broad-based enhancement of human capabilities and achievements. Capabilities provide sets of feasible alternatives for the realization of human agency. Developmental achievements include the following: growth, equity, education, health care, infrastructure, government capacity, rule-of-law, accountability, and broad political and economic access.

Second, *Collective-action problems* (CAPs) arise when individuals or organizations, following their interests and inclinations, generate undesirable outcomes for larger groups. Examples include pollution, crime, war, corruption, and climate change. There are two basic types. *First-order CAPs* concern variations of free-riding with respect to providing public goods, addressing externalities, and/or limiting uses of common resources – all broadly defined to include economic, political, and social interactions. Social peace is a public good. Excess conflict generates negative externalities. Within organizations, managerial time is a common resource. Resolving first-order CAPs entails negotiating distributions of the costs and benefits of achieving cooperation. Will the participants honor such agreements? *Second-order CAPs* concern arranging sufficient coordination and enforcement to render first-order agreements credible and thus implementable. Why should parties follow stated commitments, such as contributing to public goods or limiting pollution, when cutting corners costs less? The Kyoto climate accords foundered on this very problem.[15]

The under-utilized concept of second-order CAPs links economic and political reasoning. It provides a conceptual foundation for political economy. Exchange requires credible enforcement of agreements, and enforcement entails exercising power. Second-order CAPs thus underlie developmental dilemmas and policy failures – because distributions of power influence prospects for enforcing agreements. Indeed, if power were not embedded in these dynamics, there would be no need for policy.[16]

Third, I define power as follows: Party A's *power* is its ability to influence the incentives facing one or more other parties (B) and/or alter B's understanding of such incentives – doing so in a manner that tilts B's activities in directions favorable to A.[17] Incentives may be material (money, time, goods, services), social (reputation), or political (position).

---

[15] Bardhan (2005) notes two related types of CAPs: free-rider problems of sharing costs of inducing change; bargaining problems where disputes may undermine coordination.

[16] As North (1990) points out, Ronald Coase failed to identify the most important component of transaction costs: the costs of enforcing agreements.

[17] From Ferguson (2020, 137), combining ideas from Dahl (1957), Taylor (1982), and Lukes (1974).

Fourth, as "rules of the game" *institutions* are mutually understood behavioral prescriptions that convey expectations of relatively broad adherence.[18] Institutions may be informal, as in conventions and social norms, or formal, as in regulations and laws.

On these grounds, this Element offers the following core statement: resolving developmental dilemmas entails addressing myriad first- and second-order CAPs. Resolution, across hundreds, thousands, even millions of agents, relies on complex combinations of functional informal and formal institutions. Powerful agents, who derive their positions from prior institutional history as well as recent political contestation, endeavor to shape the operation and evolution of institutions in their favor – because they can. Indeed, institutions affect the material, political, and social outcomes they care about. Compounding CAPs of unequal influence and skewed distribution follow. Dynamic concoctions of power, agency, rules, responses, and understandings of interests, propriety, and identity thus shape and emerge from developmental dilemmas.

Functional developmental policy builds on understanding the principles of power and agency that drive such dilemmas, with attention to specific social contexts. How can we remove developmental barriers without first comprehending them?

This Element's discussion proceeds as follows.

Section 2 outlines a systematic theory of power. It notes power's sources, instruments, manifestations, and three domains of exercise (or faces; Lukes, 1974). It proceeds to triadic power – that is, power involving at least three poles of interaction or categories of participants, such as labor, management, and finance. A triadic approach facilitates understanding subtle power asymmetries and attendant externalities. Powerful agents exercise triadic power by using seven basic triadic formats (strategic templates), such as divide-and-rule (Ferguson, 2020, 2024).

Section 3, after relating structure to agency, focuses on three overlapping types of agency: leadership, following, and brokerage. It notes characteristics, activities, and relations to social context – including distributions of power – along with interactions, such as those between leaders and followers.

Section 4 discusses a fourth, broader type of agency: institutional entrepreneurship, which combines leadership and brokerage within two overlapping modes of operation. *Political-economic entrepreneurship* strives to change the rules of political-economic engagement, such as the definitions and implications of property rights and rules of participation and associated understandings

---

[18] Unenforced laws are not institutions; the attendant second-order CAP is unresolved.

of interests. *Normative-identity entrepreneurship* strives to alter interpretations of and/or the evolution of social norms and corresponding concepts of social identity. Internalized norms influence identities, and group identities foster group-specific norms. Norms and identities shape understandings of social environments, including social roles and perceptions of permitted or proscribed behavior. The section concludes by noting that singular, as opposed to pluralistic social identities, generate social cleavages and inter-group conflict.

Section 5 opens by considering how institutional entrepreneurs exercise power to promote social cleavage and conflict, using a stylized sequence and model. It follows with a rough script for countermeasures that could improve developmental outcomes. Subsequent discussion contrasts the developmental experiences of Somaliland and Somalia, as an illustration of how this Element's core principles relate to developmental policy. The conclusion reviews how this systematic approach to power and agency facilitates inquiry into the roots and consequences of developmental dilemmas operating within specific areas and social contexts: a conceptual foundation for developmental policy analysis and inclusive developmental policy.

2 Institutions and Principles of Power

Why would self-interested political and economic elites expend scarce resources to construct the complex institutions required to implement initiatives in areas such as technical education and R and D?

Richard Doner and Ben Ross Schneider, 2020

After the Second World War, development in Thailand stalled because fractured elites, already divided over relations to the prior collaborationist government, faced no compelling reasons to unify. They experienced no commonly understood threat to their political survival. Consequently, they encountered little incentive to undertake the difficult steps of establishing coherent administrative, political, and economic institutions. Instead, they relied on short-term distributions of benefits, such as low taxes and cheap electricity, to placate and sow division among local populations (Slater, 2010).

Many developing countries, including Malaysia, Thailand, Mexico, Argentina, and Turkey, have encountered a *middle-income trap* – an extended period over which prevalent standards of living fail to surpass $10,000 (2005 purchasing power parity; Gil and Kharas (2015); Spence (2011)). Such economies depend on large informal sectors, wherein ad hoc personalistic identity politics undermines class solidarity, provokes ethnic populism, and discourages investing in human capital. Entrenched political-economic inequality incentivizes and facilitates clientelism and stasis. Ultimately, the "trap" reflects developmental collective-action problems (CAPs). It exhibits political disarticulation based on unequal power combined with a failure to establish cross-coalition collective action that could motivate investments in functional institutions and structural transformation (Rodrik, 2014).

Resolving developmental dilemmas and associated collective-action problems (CAPs) relies on configurations of informal and formal institutions – and responses of myriad variously placed agents. New CAPs, such as those related to reform, ensue. In all such cases, powerful agents endeavor to tilt the evolution and operation of institutions in directions they believe match their goals – because they can. And others follow. *Political elites* – that is, agents with disproportionate power and influence on political-economic development – seek political survival (Doner et al., 2005). Elite survival requires building supporting coalitions that may facilitate resolving second-order CAPs of coordination and enforcement. For given levels of influence, elites strive to minimize coalition size to economize on distributing benefits (Riker, 1962). Accordingly, the power dynamics of political survival and distribution, as they interact with informal and formal institutions, shape developmental trajectories.

Because distributions of power underlie institutional evolution and developmental prospects, potential beneficiaries of inclusive development face multiple CAPs. Second-order CAPs of establishing credible enforcement undermine the credibility of inclusive contractual, political, and policy arrangements or agreements – and implementation. Crafting credible commitments relies on the workings and often ambiguous viability of multifaceted layers of informal and formal institutions interacting with exercises of power by variously placed agents.

A systematic approach to the elusive concept of power can, therefore, shed light on these developmental dilemmas. Following a brief discussion of institutions, this section develops such an approach. Sections 3 and 4 relate these dynamics to agency.

2.1 Institutions

Recall, institutions are "the rules of the game" in society. They are mutually understood behavioral prescriptions with anticipated observance among relevant groups. As such, institutions accomplish three basic social tasks – all related to exercising and channeling power:[19]

i. Institutions shape motivation by providing incentives and by influencing preferences. A cigarette tax can reduce smoking. Social norms that prescribe fair behavior often alter preferences.

---

[19] Ferguson (2013) elaborates on these three points.

ii. Institutions shape sources and transmissions of information. Who writes and who receives the treasurer's report?
iii. Institutions shape cognition. Their understood behavioral prescriptions outline shared mental models. Institutions establish common conceptual frameworks that facilitate interpreting social contexts (Denzau and North, 1994).[20] Who can or cannot, should or should not do what, when, and how? A simple norm against cutting in line frames understandings of how to behave when approaching a queue of, say, 100 strangers at an office or theatre. Go to the back, as those arriving before you did.

The motivational, informational, and cognitive sway institutions offer inviting avenues of influence for those able to harness and modify their prescriptions. Powerful agents thus endeavor to slant institutional evolution in directions that favor their agendas and interests, albeit sometimes mistakenly. Accordingly, skewed distributions of power condition multiple contested interactions that influence the viability, reach, and inclusiveness of political and economic institutions – along with political-economic outcomes, such as allotments of opportunity and benefit. Indeed, developmental trajectories follow cycles of disproportionate influence, contestation, and response. Sections 3–5 elaborate. I now outline a systematic approach to conceptualizing power.

2.2 Power

Recall that *power* is the ability of one party (A; an individual, organization, or functional coalition) to influence the incentives facing one or more others (B) and/or alter their understanding of such incentives – in a manner that affects their activities in directions favorable to A.[21] Bs include individuals, groups, organizations, coalitions, and populations. The incentives may be material (money, time, goods, and services), social (reputation), or political (attainment of political position).

Power has the following properties (Bowles and Gintis, 2008):

- It is social, not individual.
- Its exercise constitutes a strategic (Nash) equilibrium. For relevant agents, exercising power or submitting to it is at least as good as perceived feasible alternatives.
- Power is normatively indeterminate. It can generate positive-sum gains (Pareto improvement) or exploit victims. Parental exercises of power (e.g.,

---

[20] This Element's Section 3.1 elaborates on mental models.
[21] Ferguson 2020, 137, combining ideas from Dahl (1957), Taylor (1982) & Lukes (1974). Related: "A's power consists simply in the ability to obtain low-cost compliance from B" Bardhan (2005, 40).

Table 1 Elements of power relations

1. Sources	2. Instruments	3. Domains (faces) (Lukes, 1974)	4. Manifestations
1) Access to resources	1) Sanctions	1) Behavior, given rules	1) de facto
2) Institutionally designated positions	2) Manipulative communication	2) Rules, expectations, access	2) de jure
3) Resolution of organizational CAPs		3) Preferences & beliefs about conflict	

no dessert unless you eat your vegetables) can benefit children. Likewise, when professors grade students, they exert power. This positive vs. zero-sum distinction is important. Zero-sum perceptions of power and interests underlie debilitating social cleavages and inter-group conflict (Levy and Fukuyama, 2010).

Table 1 outlines four core elements of power relations:

Elaborating on Column 1's Sources of power:[22] Resources include money, goods, services, and information. Institutional positions may be informal, as community leaders or village chiefs, or formal, as in chairs of legislative committees or CEOs. Regarding the resolution of organizational CAPs, coherent organizations exert more power than dysfunctional ones.

Regarding Column 2's Instruments of power: Sanctions may be positive (rewards) or negative (punishments), and either implicit from preexisting context or newly introduced, as in promises and threats. *Manipulative communication* connotes forms of deception, such as lying.

Regarding Column 3's Domains of power: *Power1* entails assembling force or bargaining strength in a context with given, understood rules. It directly impacts behavior. Examples include the size of already engaged Russian and

---

[22] Bardhan (2005) notes related power sources: resource access, information asymmetry, and the ability to coordinate. In wars of attrition, power flows to the party with higher reneging costs because it would experience lower net benefits from conceding. Williamson (1979) offers a caveat on resources and power: relationship-specific resources may be subject to holdup. For Dahl (1957), one may quantify A's power with the probability that B performs some action in response to A. Harsanyi (1977) notes that this relation depends on A's cost of exercising power relative to B's cost of refusal. Similarly, Chamberlain and Kuhn (1965) define bargaining power in terms of the relative costs of agreement and disagreement facing two negotiating parties.

Ukrainian armies, the size of established voting blocs, or the amounts of money offered in already announced bribes. *Power2* alters various rules of engagement and corresponding expectations concerning responses of other parties. Power2 is equivalent to strategic moves in game theory (Schelling, 1960). Examples include issuing unanticipated threats, barring access to meetings, limiting or expanding rights of participation or voting, and altering agendas.[23] *Power3*: alters understandings and preferences regarding conflict. Party A may convince B that B wants what A wants; that a person or group in B's position should never challenge one of A's position (how dare you!); or that another party (C) is the culprit for B's problems.

Regarding Column 4's Manifestations of Power: *de facto power* signifies immediate on-the-ground power, such as the number of Russian troops facing Ukrainian troops in the Donbas in June 2023 or the number of protesters in Tahrir Square, Cairo, on 21 January 2011. In contrast, *de jure power* tends to endure, at least over medium-term time horizons. It is institutionalized, based on accepted law, regulations, or established procedures. South Korea's post-Second World War land reform altered both agricultural production and the distribution of power.

Efforts to reform, reconstruct, create, or abolish institutions utilize powers 2 and 3 with hopes to achieve de facto manifestation by institutionalizing certain behavioral prescriptions. Section 4 addresses the role of institutional entrepreneurs in such endeavors.

Because power resides in engagements, conceptualizing its exercise requires positing relevant axes or poles of interaction. Traditional approaches assume dyadic relationships. Herein, A's power influences B and vice versa without involving or affecting other parties (C). Many treatments of union-management bargaining envision dyadic exchanges. While useful, such approaches often understate power asymmetries and ignore subtle relations to third parties.[24]

In contrast, triadic conceptions of power involve at least three poles of interaction – three categories of participants, such as landlord, tenant-laborer, and merchant (Basu, 2000). Here, A↔B interactions involve, affect, or respond to the presence of third parties (Cs): power externalities. Dyads thus become bilateral components of triadic relations (A↔B; B↔C, C↔A). Triadic approaches permit the following elements (Simmel, 1902):

---

[23] See also Bachrach and Baratz (1962).
[24] An analogy: dyadic power conceptions resemble partial equilibria; triadic approaches facilitate general equilibrium analysis.

- Potential majorities
- Unclear attribution of responsibility. With incomplete observation, each party could blame the consequences of its actions on another party
- Roles for intermediaries: mediators, facilitators, "middlemen"
- Strategic manipulation of dyadic relations, whereby A (B or C) influences dyadic interactions B↔C, C↔A, or A↔B.

Exercises of triadic power operate via seven, sometimes overlapping strategic templates or *triadic power formats*. These are:[25]

- *F1: Threatening to disrupt interactions between others.*
  Landlord A threatens to block tenant-laborer B's exchanges with merchant C unless B accepts a wage below its reservation wage (Basu, 2000). Figure 1 illustrates. A thus *exploits* B, paying less than a minimal non-coerced wage offer. More generally, A may threaten to ostracize B for refusing an offer or directive. For example, community leaders may credibly threaten members with expulsion for violating local norms or commands. This dynamic also operates in areas with a single large employer, such as a mine or factory ("one-company towns"), informal employment relationships, or political coercion.
  Following the July 2016 failed coup in Turkey, President Erdoğan's government fired and blacklisted thousands of civil servants accused of sympathies with the Gülen movement, effectively denying them employment and access to many economic relationships.

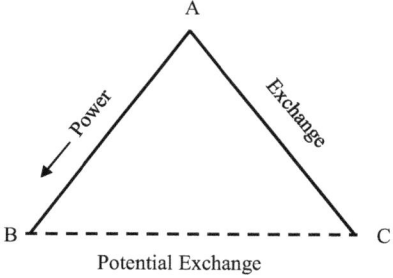

Figure 1 A format 1 power triad

Source: Adapted from Basu (2000, 6.1, 149).
Legend: A = Landlord
B = Tenant Laborer
C = Merchant/Financier

---

[25] These formats appear in Ferguson (2020, 2024), based on Simmel (1902).

- *F2: Using a 3rd party to punish or reward an adversary.*
  Dictator A hires security agents (Cs) to punish dissidents (Bs). Politician A hires assistants (Cs) to reward loyalists (Bs).

  Vladimir Putin enlisted the Wagner Group to fight in Ukraine and to promote Russian interests in African countries.
- *F3: Demanding a return for taking sides.*
  Small party or coalition A demands a powerful post, such as a ministry, in exchange for tipping the balance between larger parties B and C. This dynamic can apply to ethnic or regional conflicts.

  South Sudanese prophet Nyachol sided with former South Sudanese vice president Riek Machar and General James Koahg as they fought against President Salva Kirr's government. In return, Koang gave her cattle "as a sign of his support and allegiance" (Hutchinson and Pendle, 2015, 427).
- *F4: Divide and rule.*
  Colonist or dictator A incites ethnic, racial, religious, ideological, or resource conflict between groups B and C to undermine, control, or coerce them.[26]

  In northern Uganda, the central government undercuts locally based power by practicing *institutional arbitrariness*. It promotes local armed security groups, giving them ambiguous responsibility for maintaining order, and it randomly punishes them for undefined excesses. This arbitrary use of violence shifts rules of engagement (power2), "thereby fragmenting resistance and reinforcing its authority" (Tapscott, 2017, 264).
- *F5: Mediation.*
  Party A arbitrates B↔C disputes or negotiations. A's approach ranges from impartial to biased. Impartial mediation can benefit a larger group (D) by reducing disruptive conflict – a positive-sum outcome. Yet, the greater A's bias, the more likely it will tilt its mediation to its own advantage, reducing or eliminating positive-sum gains.[27]

  In Pakistan's Panj province, business agents, unions, and civic organizations – acting as intermediaries between political patrons and local populations – engage in *isomorphic activism*. They not only make themselves indispensable and benefit from access to various services, they also undermine democratic potential as they truncate opportunities and discourage practices of broader participation (Kirk, 2024).
- *F6: Benefiting from the mere presence of third parties.*
  Parties A and B engage in an exchange for which uninvolved Cs would replace Bs, given the opportunity. Here, A can use the existence of Cs as

---

[26] F4 differs from F1's threatened interference because exchange partners are rarely adversaries.
[27] Policy brokers mediate (Sabatier and Jenkins-Smith, 1998).

20 Development Economics

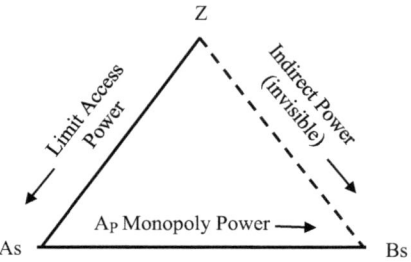

Figure 2 A format 7 power triad

Source: Ferguson 2020, 148.
Legand: Z = gatekeeper, Ap= privileged As

leverage in negotiations with Bs. For example, unemployment allows employers to credibly threaten workers with dismissal should they demand higher wages. This dynamic indicates the *short-side power* conferred by occupying certain positions in contested exchange relations, such as that of employers (Bowles and Gintis, 1992).[28]

A similar short-side power dynamic applies to attaining formal employment in settings of developmental dualism with rural-urban migration (Harris and Todaro, 1970) and to the power of financiers, positioned as creditors (Bowles, 1985; Stiglitz, 1987). Likewise, F6, perhaps combined with F3 or F4, can influence political bargaining.

- *F7: Gatekeeping* (Oleinik, 2016).

Gatekeeper, Z, limits access to desirable positions within economic, political, or social arenas. Remaining agents fit triadic categories A–C. Qualified agents (As) compete for access, but only some achieve privileged entry (A_ps); the remainder (A_us) become either Bs or Cs. Bs, such as consumers, voters, or political clients, desire transactions with As. Cs, lacking sufficient wealth, privilege, connection, or status, cannot transact in the arena. Figure 2 illustrates.

Gatekeeping power enters in three distinct fashions. First, gatekeeper Z directly exerts powers 1 and 2 over the As, as in forcefully blocking entrance into a political-economic arena or altering the rules of access. Second, by limiting the number of A_ps, Z truncates Bs' choice sets among transactions with potentially competing As. This limit alters various rules of exchange: power2. Moreover, such gatekeeping often reflects *invisible power*: the Bs may not even know of Z's existence. Third, privileged A_ps apply F6 short-side

---

[28] *Contested exchange* occurs with incomplete contracting, whereby contracts cannot fully specify the future actions of participants whose interests do not fully align, and observation is costly and incomplete (Bowles and Gintis, 1992).

power as they interact with Bs, who now face a combination of limited choice sets and the presence of many Cs who would gladly replace them.

The northern Uganda example noted under F4's divide and rule also exhibits F7 gatekeeping. The Ugandan government (Z) arbitrarily limits access to permitted enforcement activities: randomized gatekeeping. Local security groups (alternately A_ps and A_us) thus operate in an unpredictable arena that prevents them from organizing opposition to the government. Local residents, arbitrarily Bs or Cs, face unpredictably limited choices among security arrangements (Tapscott, 2017).

More broadly, gatekeeping applies to multiple developmental relationships. Table 2 lists several.

The seven formats often overlap and interact. They unfold in various combinations and sequences. For example, *interlocked credit and tenancy markets* merge agricultural tenancy, sharecropping, and debt-peonage (Stiglitz and Weiss, 1981). Landholders and merchants restrict access to credit (F7) either by occupying a dual role as financiers or, as in F1, by blocking exchanges with financiers for tenants who fail to accept exploitative remuneration. A combination of low remuneration and external events, such as natural disasters or reduced commodity prices, pushes tenants into debt that must be repaid with labor and produce, indicating *bonded labor* and debt-peonage. Moreover, the presence of unemployed rural laborers reinforces landholder short-side power (F6). Furthermore, the presence of unemployment may allow landholders, financiers, and formal employers to sow division between the employed and the unemployed or between those with better and worse land or jobs – often exacerbating social cleavages along ethnic, racial, and/or regional lines (F4). Finally, bonded labor and other exploitative arrangements may be enforced by hired managers, police, or local vigilantes (F2).

A related example illustrates long-term developmental consequences. In the post-bellum US South's system of sharecropping, [the] "merchant forced the farmer into exclusive production of cotton by refusing credit to those who sought to diversify production." The merchant's local land monopoly underlay its power to influence political and economic relationships, establishing "the roots of Southern poverty" (Ransom and Sutch 2001, 127, 149–199).

These exercises of the seven triadic formats rely on asymmetric access to power's three sources – resources, institutional positions, and the ability to resolve organizational CAPs. To secure and sustain economic and political advantage, political and business elites utilize power's instruments of sanctions and manipulative communication – with short-term de facto and longer-term de jure manifestations. They utilize power2 alterations of rules, and power3

Table 2 Developmental gatekeeping relationships and parties[a]

Interaction	Party Z	Competing As	Affected Bs	Cs
Formal-sector employment (developmental dualism)	Employers Government patrons	Urban laborers A_{P_s} get formal employment.	Rural-urban migrants Unemployed urban workers	Unemployed
Urban housing	Landlords	Tenants A_{P_s} get apartments	Tenants Homeless Migrants	Homeless Potential migrants
Retail corruption (bribes for access to goods, services, permits)	Owners or government agents	Potential owners or government agents A_{P_s} get contracts or jobs	Consumers or applicants	The poor
Patronage	Patrons: Monopolists, Resource owners, Politicians, Government agents	Businesses Politicians Government agents A_{P_s} receive benefits	Clients: Businesses Consumers Citizens	Citizens who lack resources or connections Aspiring entrepreneurs
Monopoly entry	Powerful firms, Government agents	Businesses Entrepreneurs A_{P_s} gain entry	Businesses Entrepreneurs	Citizens

			Citizens
Resource access	Landowners, including government agencies & foreign interests	Resource developers: Aspiring businesses Political and economic entrepreneurs A_{Ps} gain access	Resource users: Consumers Businesses Entrepreneurs Potential patrons Ethnic groups	
Selective property-right enforcement	Patrons (as above)	Businesses, asset holders, citizens A_{Ps} receive ordered deals (enforced)	Businesses, asset holders, citizens	Lower-status citizens Informal enterprises

[a] These transactions exhibit both positive- and zero-sum properties, depending on the axis of exchange.

reinterpretation of conflict – often exercised via combinations of triadic formats. Such maneuvers establish conditions for concurrent or subsequent direct application of force (power1). Combined exercises of power shape institutional trajectories, developmental dilemmas, associated CAPs, and ultimately, political settlements – by applying agency to structure. Section 3's topic.

3 Foundations of Structural Change: Three Types of Agency

He who wishes to be obeyed must know how to command.
Niccolo Machiavelli

'... *others mediated between these figures [patrons] and those lower down, bridging these separate worlds while simultaneously deriving benefits from keeping them some distance apart.*'

Deborah James, 2011

How did South Africans resolve the dilemma of transforming the apartheid system into a multi-racial democracy? They organized opposition. Their escape from apartheid emerged from the combined and evolving influences of many participants, including leadership from Nelson Mandela and Desmund Tutu; militant opposition with broad following; additional leadership, organizing, and brokerage, from the African National Congress (ANC), Confederation of South African Trade Unions (COSATU), and the South African Anglican Church; international sanctions; and F.W. de Klerk's willingness to negotiate with Mandela. Multidimensional agency overturned structure.

Section 2 established a systematic approach to conceptualizing how powerful agents influence developmental trajectories. Recall, powerful agents may be individuals, organizations, or functional coalitions. Their influence operates within evolving contexts of institutions, common understandings, and patterns of behavior. Well-positioned and resourced elites operating within historically inherited structures pursue political-economic goals using power to exercise agency that can – intentionally or not – transform structure.

This section's discussion proceeds as follows. Section 1 relates *agency* to *structure*. Section 2 addresses cognitive foundations of agency based on bounded rationality and shared mental models. Section 3 discusses three basic types of agency: leadership, following, and brokerage, with attention to basic concepts, activities, and interactions. On this basis, Section 4 will address a hybrid type of agency: institutional entrepreneurship.

3.1 Agency and Structure

Agency is simply the exercise of rationalizable choice concerning intentional action in pursuit of goals (Battilana et al. 2014; Corbett, 2019; Grillitsch and

Sotaruta, 2020). How do agents perceive, make sense of, or justify their decisions within specific contexts populated with myriad actors, actions, practices, and anticipated responses? They may consider ethical principles and consequences regarding material gain, desired positions, and reputation. *Structure* refers to the relatively durable contours of contexts within which agents interact, including informal and formal institutions, established habits, and corresponding culturally inherited conceptual frameworks that shape understandings of social and physical environments.

Structure and agency coevolve. Structure establishes both constraints on and opportunities for individual and group activity and thought. Agency shapes the contentious and disjointed evolution of structure via complex shifting, competing, conflicting, and cooperative activities of multiple participants – endowed with different understandings, capabilities, interests, and unequal power (Leftwich, 2010). Powerful agents exert disproportionate influence. They employ power's three domains and seven triadic formats in efforts to shape political-economic outcomes and the contested trajectories of institutional change. Yet, outcomes frequently evade intention. Deliberate structural change, as in political-economic reform, thus presents formidable collective-action problems (CAPs).

"Institutions are the rules of the game in a society" (North, 1990, 3). Accordingly, game theory can illustrate the co-evolution of structure and agency as a foundation for understanding the shaping of institutions and developmental consequences. The rules of a game specify who plays, possible actions, the timing of moves, what players know or do not know, all possible outcomes, and the payoffs at each. Payoffs can be material (money, time, goods, services), social (reputation), and political (access to position). Establishing structure constitutes a pre-game whose outcome depends on applications of agency within various deliberate, unintended, and random interactions among agents with different motivations and unequal influence (Aoki, 2001). *Pre-games* create rules (structure) for subsequent games within which more broadly dispersed and less scripted applications of agency generate proximate outcomes – such as distributions of resources and benefits. Over time, accumulated reactions spawn new pre-games: new structures for future encounters. The process repeats. A mix of unequal exercises of agency based on asymmetric distributions of power and chance thus shapes the creation, sustenance, alteration, and abolition of institutional structures – often with unintended consequences. Developmental dilemmas with varying prospects for resolution follow.

Macro structures condition these dynamics. Here are two conceptualizations. First, *institutional systems* are interactive combinations of institutions and organizations: institutions as rules; organizations as players. Institutions prescribe behavioral patterns that, when adopted, configure arenas for interaction. Organizations act. *Organizations* are structured groupings that operate roughly as a unit. They pursue sets of negotiated goals using evolving decision rules to understand and coordinate key operations (Cyert and March, 1963). Institutional prescriptions point to resolutions of first-order CAPs by indicating who should contribute how much, and so forth. But, due to second-order CAPs, institutions alone do not generate cooperation. Organizations coordinate activity and dispense enforcement that can resolve second-order CAPs. Institutional systems thus deliver behavioral outcomes, albeit imperfectly, with unintended consequences. Between 1947 and 1990, the institutional system of Eastern European communism employed multiple rules, such as state ownership of productive facilities, with enforcement via security organizations, such as East Germany's Stasi.

Second, at a more foundational level, political settlements shape institutional evolution and attendant dilemmas. As ongoing, often informal, mutual understandings among powerful actors to rely on politics rather than organized violence for addressing internal disputes, *political settlements* shape institutional development and distributions of benefits. They condition prospects for resolving developmental CAPs – and create new ones.[29] For example, a settlement with a broad social foundation and an incoherent configuration of power indicates rough amalgams of disparate insider groups who, having failed to resolve internal organizational CAPs, pursue disjointed agendas. An ensuing developmental dilemma concerns how to coherently allocate policy authority without narrowing the social foundation's breadth by excluding formerly included groups. India offers an example. A broad social foundation has included Hindus, Muslims, and Sikhs – albeit with unequal influence – interacting with disjointed authority, and no consensus on major issues such as the role of religion in the state. The current government appears to be concentrating power and narrowing the social foundation by marginalizing Muslims (Mody, 2023).

Agency thus operates within macro structures of institutional systems based on political settlements that, to varying degrees, shape and constrain meso-level regional, sectoral, and policy structures.

3.1.1 Cognitive Foundations of Agency

Exercising agency relies on understandings of environments, potential responses, and concurrent rationalizations. How might analysts conceptualize such reliance? In contrast to the self-centered, outcome-oriented, material-focused rationality of

---

[29] See Section 1 and Appendix 1 for a typology of political settlements.

many economic models – or even game theory's substantive-rationality approach, which can incorporate social preferences – I ground agency in bounded-rationality. As they pursue goals, agents make choices not only based on incomplete, asymmetric information, as in many economic models; they do so with limited and costly cognition.

How then might agents understand their shifting, uncertain social environments? They construct, utilize, and copy mental models. *Mental models* combine physical and social categories (e.g., tall, short, old, young, Black, White, Hindu, Muslim) with basic notions of causality. If I water a plant, it will grow. Arising from prior exposure and experience, mental models combine intuitive understandings with deliberate reasoning to generate judgments.[30] They establish conceptual underpinnings of agency.

People share mental models. Ideas that appear useful travel via narratives and symbols. *Shared mental models* exhibit common vocabularies, categories, perceived patterns, causal relationships, and implied expectations. By adopting shared mental models, individuals avoid the cognitive costs of mental innovation. Shared models spread across populations with an evolutionary selection dynamic. People copy ideas that appear good or successful and discard apparently bad, unsuccessful ones. Appearances, however, can deceive. Cognitive efficiency notwithstanding, shared mental models often underlie systematic error and bias.

Even so, mental models foster two types of adaptive learning. First, agents engage in hypothesis testing. They utilize causal relations from given mental models to evaluate outcomes. Second, following sufficient inconsistencies, they engage in difficult *re-evaluative learning*. They discard old and develop new mental models (Kahneman, 2003). Because reevaluation requires costly cognitive effort, mental models exhibit a punctuated-equilibrium dynamic: relatively long periods of stability based on hypothesis testing with occasional bursts of reevaluation. Before a revolution, dissidents may experiment with efforts at reform. Sufficient failure can, however, shift their conceptions of social change.

Shared mental models coordinate understandings in uncertain environments. They resolve cognitive free-rider problems of constructing conceptual frameworks that underlie collective behavioral responses. Institutions and ideologies are shared mental models (Denzau and North, 1994). As noted in Section 2, institutions frame understandings of social contexts, in addition to offering incentives and shaping conduits of information. *Ideologies are* shared mental models with ethical content that convey a vision of a "good" society that could, with sufficient effort and devotion, replace a dysfunctional (or "evil") status

---

[30] Mental models combine Kahneman's (2003) S1 and S2 mental processes.

quo. Ideologies express paradigmatic ideas that convey challenge and motivate action. Examples include a Marxist vision of a classless society and a libertarian vision of unregulated free enterprise.

Common behavioral responses rely on the cognitive frameworks provided by shared mental models. Institutions, as shared mental models, indicate *social choreography* (Gintis, 2009; Ferguson, 2019). Accordingly, the act of sharing mental models provides a conduit for exercising power. Well-positioned agents use narratives and symbols to direct group activity. Compelling narratives can become shared mental models that invoke power2 influence on rules and expected responses, along with power3 influence on understandings of conflict.

Broadly speaking, there are four interacting types of agency: leadership, following, brokerage, and institutional entrepreneurship. Any individual may exercise several types in various roles, interactions, and circumstances. This section focuses on the first three as background for Section 4's institutional entrepreneurs.

3.2 Leaders and Followers

Leaders are agents with a following. They openly mobilize people and resources to pursue their goals. Their motivations include material gain, power, a cause or ideology, a sense of obligation, recognition, redemption, and addressing a challenge or problem. Leaders see opportunities where others do not. They break rules (Bailey, 1969).[31] They provide and withhold services and information. Exercising powers 2 and 3, they issue directives, define issues, and shape understandings by converting their perceptions and proclivities into shared mental models. To exercise power 1, they often recruit others (triadic power format 3).

How does one become a leader? By attracting followers via physical or cognitive influence. Leaders need backing and legitimacy, based on roughly congruent goals, such as avoiding bad outcomes or compatible identities. Leadership capacity depends on personal characteristics, relations to followers, prior actions, and access power's three sources, notably positions in social networks – all conditioned by historically inherited social context, understandings, and chance. Leaders may make history, but not under conditions they choose. Gandhi did not choose British colonialism.

Followers obey, imitate, conform to, or acquiesce to various directives, commands, signaled expectations, or actions of leaders, rules, or systems. They are members of populations – often victims – and sometimes rule

---

[31] Most leaders are not elites. *Elites*, some of whom are brokers, disproportionately influence policy.

enforcers or visible operators within middle layers of hierarchies. Security services play this dual role. Follower motivations include loyalty, material and social benefit, and self-preservation. They respond to cues, including subtle signals, force, threats, and the framing of issues and contexts in shared mental models – as well as their own inclinations. Yet, even their preferences respond to leader signals, anticipated responses from other followers, and social rules or expectations.[32] Followers internalize behavioral patterns and prescriptions garnered from prior experience, social context, and leader-follower activity. Followers also choose between competing leaders. These acts of following, even submission to coercion, involve agency.

How does one become a follower? By deciding to obey, copy, conform, or refrain from criticism. Followers make choices under constraints related to feasible action and the perceived consequences of not following. Understandings of such alternatives influence propensities to follow – as opposed to resisting, ignoring, or leading. These interactions, moreover, reflect positions in social networks, associated hierarchies, and power relationships.

3.2.1 Leader-Follower Dynamics

Leader-follower relationships are political. Leaders need to attract followers. Followers exercise discretion.

Figure 3 illustrates several pathways of leader-follower interactions.

First, consider leaders. Two types of relationships arise:

1. Potential leaders (A and B) compete for followers. They signal their qualifications as well as directives to followers in response to anticipated follower reactions.
2. Powerful agents, including leaders, rely on others to enforce directives because they lack the physical capability for sanctioning broad disobedience (Hobbes, 1668). Enforcement becomes a type of following that sustains leaders.

A feedback dynamic ensues. Leaders act. Followers observe, evaluate, and respond. Leaders observe, evaluate, and respond, and so forth. Reciprocal relationships and exchange obligations develop. Herein, followers may or may not express and act on their preferences. Leaders may or may not face incentives to respond.

Now consider three interacting follower dynamics: coercion, conformity, and assessments of competing leaders. I address these in order.

---

[32] Preferences are endogenous to social contexts (e.g., Bowles, 1998).

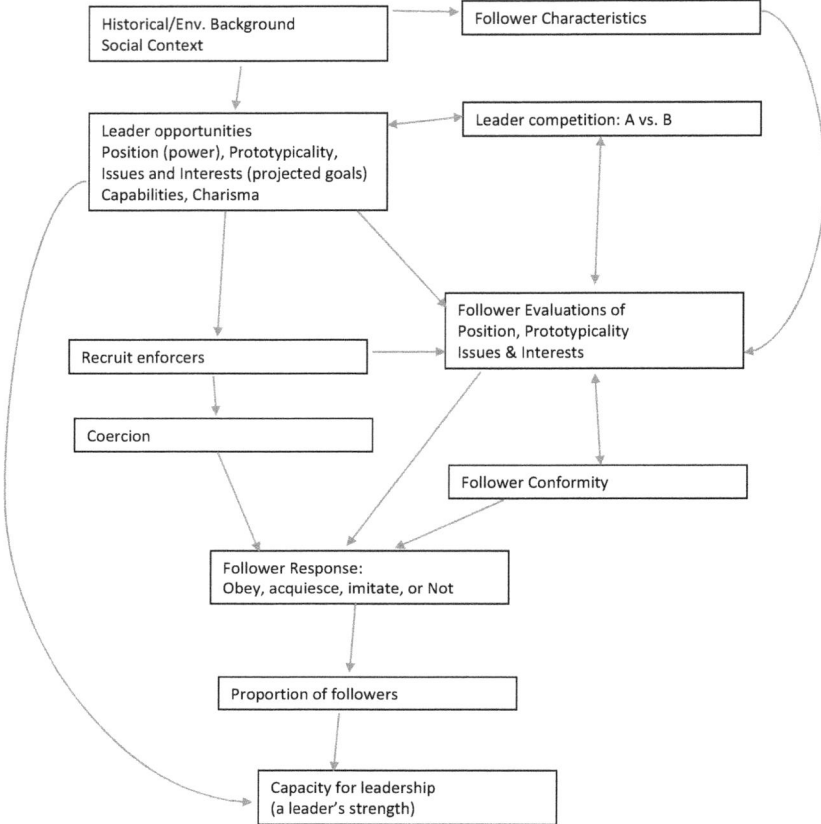

Figure 3 Leader-follower interactions

First dynamic, coercion: Leaders, often via enforcers (triadic format 2), coerce followers. They employ or arrange direct sanctions (power1), threatened sanctions (power2), and manipulative communication that alters perceptions of potential leader-follower conflict and related preferences (power3).

Second dynamic, conformity: Social pressure to conform arises from observed or expected following among others in similar contexts (Hume). Figure 4, a multiplayer game of assurance, illustrates. Here, an expected group proportion of followers (η) influences an agent's social/material payoffs (ω_i) that accompany two possible strategies: obey the leader's directive ($O(\eta)$), or disobey ($D(\eta)$).

Assume homogeneous members of group G. The $O(\eta)$ and $D(\eta)$ curves depict how a marginal individual's payoff (ω_i) responds to strategies D and O as η increases. With an initial equilibrium at $\eta = 0$, the $D(\eta)$ intercept (D_0) sits above

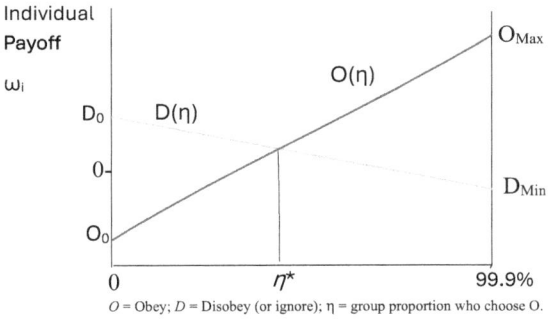

Figure 4 Multiplayer following game

the $O(\eta)$ intercept O_0. Current social/material incentives discourage following. The negative $D(\eta)$ and positive $O(\eta)$ slopes, however, imply that increases in η enhance the net social pressure to obey. Value η^*, an unstable Nash equilibrium, signifies a tipping point: the minimum expected proportion of followers that would incentivize obedience. Below η^*, social incentives motivate O, and vice versa. Additionally, both curves shift in response to changes in social context as well as leader influence on follower expectations and understandings of conflict – via powers2 and 3. Notably, given other factors, any $\eta > \eta^*$ engenders leadership.

Combined pressure from coercion and conformity often induces *preference falsification*. Followers confront tradeoffs between their private goals, on the one hand, and the perceived net social/material benefits from public expression of conformist activity, on the other (Kuran, 1995). Might one publicize one's opposition to a leader or regime?

Third dynamic, evaluation: Following relies on assessments of the characteristics and influence of potential leaders within pertinent social contexts. Evaluations respond to four leader attributes: position, interests, issues, and identity.[33]

i. *Position:* Connections with influential public-and private-sector actors and access to resources underlie a leader's potential impact.
ii. *Interests*: The degree to which followers believe a leader cares about their interests.
iii. *Issues*: Visible pursuit of issues followers care about can foster trust.
iv. *Prototypicality*: The degree to which a potential leader shares a group's social identity (e.g., ethnicity) bolsters trust and creates margins for error. Prototypical leaders enjoy leeway to fail, break rules, and even compromise

---

[33] This discussion follows the PIII framework of Hudson and McLaughlin (2019).

follower interests – without loss of authority. In contrast, non-prototypical leaders may lack legitimacy, even after success. Gandhi's successful inclusive approach to opposing British colonialism did not appeal to sectarian Hindus – as evidenced by his assassination and the subsequent partition of India and Pakistan.

Russian President Vladimir Putin exhibits prototypical leadership. By projecting a vision of Russian ethnic/national social identity, he has garnered the appearance of concern for popular interests and issues. He enjoys leeway. War casualties and Ukrainian drone strikes within Russia have not diminished public expressions of support. Regarding coercion, Putin has punished evaders (power1), introduced legal conscription (power2), and blamed the Ukraine war on the West – with implied disloyalty for not following his directives (power3).

Now consider a general model. Applying a few equations to Figure 4 can illustrate leader-follower interactions. In addition to conformity pressure denoted by the slopes of the $O(\eta)$ and $D(\eta)$ curves, follower tradeoffs respond to coercion and follower assessments of competing leaders. In Figure 4, the D_0 and O_0 intercepts become variables that respond to leader prototypicality, coercion, charisma, and sources of power (position) within a given environment. Assume competing leaders J and K. Disobeying leader J connotes obeying K. We have:

$$O_J = O_J(\eta_J; PR_{JK}, C_{JK}; CH_{JK}; SP_{JK}; ENV); \text{ and} \qquad (1)$$

$$D_J \equiv O_K = O_K(\eta_K; PR_{JK}, C_{JK}; CH_{JK}; SP_{JK}; ENV) \qquad (2)$$

η_J = J's proportionate following; PR_{JK}, C_{JK}, CH_{JK}, and SP_{JK} respectively signify relative J/K prototypicality, coercion, charisma, and sources of power (position); ENV = social environment.

Changes in these arguments shift D_0 and O_0, moving the η^* tipping point, altering the minimal required following for effective leadership.

Reflecting this logic, equation (3) illustrates leader J's potential influence, i.e., leadership capacity:

$$L_J = L_J(\eta_{JK}; PR_{JK}, C_{JK}; CH_{JK}; SP_{JK}; ENV). \qquad (3)$$

The arguments of (1)–(3) interact and depend on the strategies of all involved. A feedback dynamic arises. An increase in η_J enhances conformity pressure for O_J, shown as movement along $D(\eta)$ and $O(\eta)$. Increases in PR_{JK}, C_{JK}, CH_{JK}, and SP_{JK} shift both $O(\eta_J)$ and $D(\eta_J)$ leftwards, pushing η_J^* closer to the origin. These impacts both rely on and enhance SP_{JK}. Over time, CH_{JK} may increase, generating reinforcing feedback. Concurrent or subsequent impacts on ENV may amplify or diminish these effects. Whenever these interactions push η_J above η_J^*, leader J attains a self-enforcing Nash equilibrium among potential followers as obedience levels approach O_{Max}.

A more complicated model could incorporate distinctions between follower groups J and K, heterogeneity among each group's members, and allow for recruitment within the other group. Additionally, conflict could augment either or both leaders' claims to prototypicality, solidifying their following, reinforcing or further enhancing conflict incentives.[34] Society may face corresponding developmental CAPs.

More comprehensively, leaders interact with followers in large social games with multiple equilibria that reflect distinct cultural practices. Applying game-theoretic reasoning to Hobbes and Hume, Basu (2021) asserts that, within such environments, sustainable leader influence relies on attaining a *deviation-proof* Nash equilibrium. Followers must perceive no feasible alternative actions that could augment their anticipated returns to following. Otherwise, leadership would unravel over time.

To illustrate leadership dynamics in such games, first consider a *focal point* – that is, one of many possible Nash equilibria upon which player expectations converge (Schelling, 1960). Whereas in principle, meetings might occur at many times and locations, a schedule signals a focal point, such as 20:00 at the village square. A leader's words and actions signal focal points from which unilateral deviation would not increase follower payoffs. Showing up at 19:00 would waste time.

A dynamic concept of leadership goes further. Leaders become *focal persons* (Basu, 2021). A *focal person* is someone followers rely on to issue strategic group decisions over time as environments and interactions change – often unexpectedly. Focal persons signal focal points in real time. They share (propagate) mental models of adaptive response. They simultaneously resolve CAPs of coordinating group behavior and cognitive free-rider problems. They save followers the mental effort of devising new strategies.

Yevgeny Prigozhin was the focal person in the short-lived Wagner Group mutiny against Russian authority. On 23 June 2023, following his directives, Wagner soldiers, who had previously engaged Ukrainian forces, crossed the Russian border to enter Rostov-on-Don – the site of the Southern Russian Military District headquarters. On 24 June, after successful encounters with Russian forces, they approached Moscow. Perhaps fearing civil war, Prigozhin ordered his troops to turn around. As Wagner's focal person, Prigozhin not only resolved a series of strategic quandaries in the unpredictable environment of armed conflict, he also shaped the troops' understandings of conflict. He blamed the

---

[34] Sections 4.3 and 4.4 elaborates on conflict and group loyalty.

Russian military establishment for failure in Ukraine's Donbas region and shifted the rules of the Wagner-Russia conflict game (powers 3 and 2). These activities and further directives fostered subsequent power1 encounters with Russian soldiers. Appendix 2 offers a pertinent signaling game.

3.2.2 Leaders and Power

Within these dynamics, power's sources, instruments, manifestations, domains, and formats shape leader influence on conflict arenas and outcomes. Table 3 summarizes.

Again, the Wagner mutiny illustrates. Prigozhin utilized power's domains. With power3, his actions and narratives signaled that no Wagner soldier should ever challenge him or a superior officer. Rules of combat followed (power2) and then armed engagement (power1). Regarding triadic formats, Prigozhin used his troops to attack Russian soldiers (F2). Before the mutiny, he sought rewards from Putin for supporting the Ukraine war (F3). During the mutiny, he sowed division among Russian soldiers and the public (F4). He likely benefited from the presence of shocked local citizens (F6). He had previously screened entry into the Wagner group (F7) and likely ostracized the excluded or disloyal (F1). Moreover, when Prigozhin ordered retreat, he responded to (the self-serving) mediation by Belarusian president Alexander Lukashenko (F5).

On a grander scale, powerful charismatic leaders invoke, interpret, and occasionally create paradigmatic ideologies, as they mix powers 2 and 3 to advance their goals. For example, as he rose to power in 1920s Italy, Benito Mussolini's political narratives framed Italian patriotism in terms of an existential conflict with foreigners, domestic leftists, and cultural degenerates. The narratives called on Mussolini's leadership, buttressed by citizen obedience and persecution of "enemies", to "purify" the nation. Other "strongmen", including Spain's Francisco Franco, Libya's Muammar Gaddafi, Zaire's Mobutu Sese Seko, and Chile's Augusto Pinochet, have used similar scripts (Ben-Ghiat, 2020).

Leader-follower dynamics interact and often overlap with brokerage.

3.3 Brokers

Brokers work behind the scenes.[35] They are facilitators, mediators, guides, negotiators, and representatives, operating with some autonomy. They are "network specialists" who inhabit or work across gaps and overlapping layers of geography, sovereignty, social practice, and systems of knowledge. Their motivations range from enabler to parasite (Goodhand and Walton, 2022).

---

[35] This discussion draws from James (2011), Kosters and Leynseele (2018), Meehan and Plonski (2017), and Wolf (1956).

Table 3 Leaders and power[a]

Sources	Position	Resources	Org. CAPs
	Informal (village chief); Formal (legislator); Local and external network connections	L's wealth, information, land, PSR	Cohesion of L's follower groups/ orgs.
Instruments	Directives with clear or implied sanctions	Manipulative communication: Stories that misinform followers or adversaries	
Manifestations	*De facto*: L leads coalitions, protests, armed conflicts, etc.	*De jure*: L uses position to issue directives, achieve compliance, shape institutional formation, and operation	
Domains	P1: L's directives convey understood sanctions (bribes, punishments)	P2: directives alter rules via new threats or promises; barring or expanding access to arenas	P3: L's narratives frame issues and perceptions of the ENV and other players to alter understandings of conflict

Table 3 (cont.)

Triadic Formats

Format 1	L threatens to block a party's exchanges with others
Format 2	L openly recruits 3rd parties to reward or punish others (e.g., security forces)
Format 3	L receives benefits from patrons or clients in exchange for support in disputes
Format 4	L creates/enhances separation or conflict among rival groups
Format 5	L openly arbitrates disputes, negotiates, directs followers to exchanges
Format 6	The presence of marginal populations strengthens L's position or legitimacy
Format 7	L's position facilitates control over access to exchanges or political arenas in a manner that reduces others' choices

Legend: L = leader; ENV = social & physical environment; PSR = point-source resources

[a] See Section 2 for details on power.

Brokers deal in power, resources, and ideas. They assemble relationships and exchanges. They reach across political, economic, and social barriers between competing interests, individuals, and groups, with contrasting perspectives, logics, discourses, and ideologies – and differential access to power. They interpret and translate. They finesse deals. They become social lubricants.

Mixing elements of patron-client and representative-constituency relationships, and operating at micro (local), meso (regional), and/or macro (center-periphery) levels, brokers act as buffers. They simultaneously create connections between distinct social domains and profit from maintaining their separation (Randeraad, 1998; James, 2011). They "transmit, direct, filter, receive, code, decode, and interpret messages" (Meehan and Plonski, 2017, citing Boissevain, 1965, 549). They render peripheral areas "legible" to the center and vice versa. This ability to straddle knowledge systems and social patterns allows brokers to serve as conduits and gatekeepers to services, land, finance, markets, legal systems, bureaucracies, businesses, NGOs, levels of governments, and external powers. Brokers are "defined by boundaries and flows of power they mediate" (Meehan and Plonski, 2017, 2). Ultimately, they influence how power is mobilized and disrupted.

Brokers may be community leaders, bureaucrats, mid-level politicians, businesspeople, attorneys, or religious figures. Notable brokerage sites include borderlands, margins of the state, semi-autonomous areas; areas of market expansion, rapid technological change, or displacement – areas of social transition.

For example, the Mexican Revolution (La Guerra Civil Mexicana, 1910–1920) destroyed the prior hacienda system of land ownership and debt-bondage, creating new relationships between shifting local communities and the incipient center of power managed by El Partido Revolucionario Institutional (the PRI). Operating as a political holding company, the PRI constructed channels for communication and mobility between dispersed communities and the center. Local brokers, operating at community margins, could "gain control of the local termini of these channels" (Wolf, 1956, 1071). They helped poor, non-Spanish-speaking residents navigate the shifting details of PRI land reform policies by connecting locals with national operatives. They gained power and recognition through "manipulation of social ties and improvisation upon them," accounting for both community and national expectations (Wolf, 1956).

Brokers manage contestation rather than resolve it. (Wolf, 1956; Stovel and Shaw, 2012; Goodhand and Walton, 2022).[36] Following South Africa's 1994 transition to democracy, the government initiated an evolving land reform program that responded to conflicting pressure for equity, black economic empowerment, and market enterprise. To navigate this terrain, rural brokers

---

[36] Section 4's bricolage, exaptation, and effectuation apply.

developed a "repertoire in the contested space between ... increasingly divergent models or ideologies of property ownership." They strived to balance conflicting central pressures with the local authority of traditional patriarchs from both the Ndebele and Pedi ethnic groups (James, 2011, 327).

3.3.1 The Supply and Demand for Brokerage

How does one become a broker? Brokerage emerges from both supply-side positions and demand-side impetus. I begin with supply.[37]

Brokerage relies on network positions: interfaces of power, resources, exchange, and communication between geographical, economic, political, social, conceptual, and ideological realms. A "structural relation linked to longer-term processes of state formation, state crises, market expansion and violent conflict" conditions broker agency (Goodhand and Walton, 2022, 2235). The functionality of and access to such positions depend on the boundaries spanned, norms, broker competition, and the type of connection.

Three types of network connections apply:

1. *Embeddedness in a peripheral community.* Brokers occupy local positions and corresponding means of communication and coercion. Their influence flows from managing connections with external businesses and central officials, who offer benefits in return for resource access or political support. For example, village chiefs or local magistrates facilitate exchanges with central officials and businesses. To survive, embedded brokers must balance local acceptability with their value to external authorities.
2. *Channels to external actors.* Brokers are "implanted in the margins" to work on behalf of external authorities (Meehan and Plonski, 39). Their influence flows from external support via coercive power, resource access, and service provision. They craft patronage relationships. In Karachi, revenue officials negotiate bribes with local land agents. To survive, implanted brokers must maintain local connections. Their capabilities ebb and flow with changes in state power, shifting boundaries, market relations, and wars.
3. *Liaison positions.* Brokers occupy social positions that bridge center and periphery. Their influence flows from straddling relationships and facilitating transactions and mobility. Examples include "middle minorities," as in Chinese traders who served as intermediaries between Dutch or Japanese colonialists and Southeast Asian populations. Broker capabilities ebb and flow with shifting external and local market and political conditions.

---

[37] This discussion draws from Meehan and Plonski (2017), Goodhand and Walton (2022), Kosters and Leynseele (2018), and Auerbach and Thachil (2018). Abstracting from horizontal relationships, I focus on vertical brokerage.

Two sources of demand for brokers interact with their network positions and influence their propensities to impose, resist, or negotiate change:

1. *Invited brokerage:* external demand

    External actors seek brokers to manage servicing clients, build electoral support, maintain (or undermine) boundaries, and contain or exacerbate conflict. Combining elements of centralism and regionalism and operating within poorly delineated policy arrangements, brokers extend patronage. They forge connections; they incorporate elites into resource-sharing pacts (Goodhand and Walton, 2022). Patron, broker, and client interests tend to coalesce around perpetuating such arrangements – extending central authority.

    Between 1300 and the 19th century, the Ottoman Empire utilized local notables for delivering and transmitting directives to local populations and authorities. Such arrangements enhanced the empire's stability. "Divide and rule, brokerage, segmentation, and integration become the basic structural components of empire." Barkley (2008, 10).

2. *Representative brokerage*: local demand

    Marginal local populations seek access to services, markets, and social or political arenas. Brokers facilitate resident activity and negotiate on their behalf. They assemble chains of exchange, memberships, and organizational hierarchy. Local parties evaluate brokers, with attention to social categories (ethnicity), external and local connections, capabilities (education, technical and organizational skills), and efficacy at tasks such as distributing services.

    Residents of Indian slums played a "meaningful role in selecting the brokers that staff electoral machines," with attention to qualifications and ethnic-political motives (Auerbach and Thachil, 2018, 775).

    Although representative brokerage gives voice to clients, it remains vulnerable to external influence.

    Moreover, unstable authority blurs distinctions between invited and representative broker demand. After the 1997 Asian financial crisis, government and migrant groups both solicited brokers to navigate transregional and transnational migration (Lindquist et al., 2012).

    The various interacting sources of supply and demand for brokerage typically generate unstable relationships.

    Brokers face recurring instability. Since their *raison d'être* arises from shifting tensions in murky environments, with fluid, incompatible demands, brokers struggle to maintain their positions. They must preserve the ability to span gaps between regions and constituencies, with disparate interests and understandings. They must balance external desires to manage, destabilize, or control peripheries with local hopes for representation. They must finesse these tensions, lest others take their place. Even when brokers deliver local opportunity and benefits, they often arouse resentment from perceptions of cooptation or profiteering – along with reprisal from authorities.

In Karachi, land brokers who negotiate service access for slum residents occupy an "apex of competing and contradictory demands" from denizens and rent-seekers, including tax collectors. Illegal arrangements rely on bribery. Resentment follows, but the community needs brokers' expertise. (Anwar, 2013, 35).

Brokered arrangements thus become "Faustian bargains" wherein "Janus-faced" brokers – juggling inconsistent requests with disjointed logics – offer different measures and justifications to different groups (Koster and van Leynseele, 2018). "Inevitably, the combining of such unlike attributes in the person of the broker presents a figure of moral uncertainty" (James, 2011, 319). Indeed, brokerage yields temporary "fixes," analogous to drug addiction (Meehan and Plonski, 2017).

3.3.2 Impacts of Brokerage

To what degree does brokerage benefit clients? To what degree does it preserve extant structures and unequal distributions? Does brokerage maintain boundaries? Does it mitigate or exacerbate conflict?

On the one hand, brokerage extends services to marginal populations and creates avenues for communication. Brokers resolve local CAPs of mobilization and achieving access to political, social, and economic arenas. They offer "the principal organized voice for the marginalized in their localities" (Goodhand and Walton, 2022, 10).

On the other hand, brokerage often disempowers periphery groups, reproducing dependency. It renders peripheries "legible" to the center. Short-term gains to clients entrench patterns of patron authority, solidifying, often informal, hierarchies, as disjointed interests coalesce around perpetuating such relationships. Both invited and representative brokerage undermine local organizational potential by splintering groups and compromising the legitimacy of coopted leaders. Brokerage thus extends tentative central authority into peripheral regions. By precluding organized resistance, it offers weak states pathways to minimal compliance and order. Lacking capacities to directly intervene, authorities delegate meddling to "ethnic frameworks" via locally embedded or centrally connected brokers. Such brokerage thus facilitates exclusionary quasi-stabilization in marginal areas (James, 2011; Meehan and Plonski, 2017).

South Africa's post-1994 land reform initiatives increasingly utilized market mechanisms. Rather than confronting risky CAPs of creating organizations, rural residents relied on brokers to navigate the shifting complexities. Residents "abdicated their potentially open access to the state and/or major markets in order to gain mediated access." (James, 2011, 319, citing Eisenstade and Roniger, 1980). Likewise, in Karachi, despite efforts to negotiate on behalf of poor residents, brokerage has facilitated tenant and squatter evictions by simplifying land acquisition for politicians and allies. Nevertheless, ensuing uncertainties reinforce resident demand for brokerage. Land masters "denote an ambiguous political agency." Such contested sovereignty becomes a form of governance. Authorities tolerate illicit broker activity to manage land settlement (Anwar, 2013, 11).

Similarly, for China, transport intermediaries, as "princely peddlers," have become an integral part of migration governance. Authorities utilize chains of agents to "transform unpredictable individual mobility into legible, aggregate flows, and to hold agents as scapegoats if needed." Brokers occupy a middle ground "where legibility and legality are produced and where regulation as social interactions is actually exercised" (Lindquist et al., 2012, 51; 68).

3.4 Brokerage, Agency, and Power

Brokerage is thus a reflection of, and a dynamic force shaping the mechanisms through which power is made mobile and space is organized

(Meehan and Plonski, 2017, 51).

Ultimately, "Brokers are not only products, but also producers, of the kind of society in which they re-emerge" (James, 2011, 319). In Karachi, broker–landowner–government–NGO interactions create "new urban forms, orderings of property and citizenship arrangements" (Anwar, 2013, 14). As myriad patrons, clients, and intermediaries demand, respond to, and exercise brokerage, they exercise agency within and across shifting constellations of center–periphery relationships structured by intermingling clusters of informal and formal institutions. Brokers assemble, bridge, or interfere with overlapping strata of local and external gatherings, communities, businesses, coalitions, organizations, and agencies. As it renders margins "legible" to external actors, brokerage escalates or deescalates violence, extends or contracts contentious boundaries, and strengthens or undermines state power. Whereas it rarely induces structural change, brokerage occasionally stabilizes partially inclusive center-periphery relationships in manners that ameliorate or exacerbate developmental dilemmas. On a grander scale, brokerage forges, sustains, and destabilizes political settlements. Power infuses such interactions.

Table 4 summarizes how the sources, instruments, manifestations, domains, and seven triadic formats of power underlie brokerage.

Table 4 Brokers and power

Sources	Network Position		Resources	Resolution of Org. CAPs
	Locally Embedded	**Connected to Center**	**Wealth, Information Point-source**	**Local groups Connections Reach of center**
Instruments	Direct or threatened sanctions re assembling or deconstructing relationships Manipulative narratives, frames, understandings of social relations			
Manifestations	De facto: fixes	De jure: emerging, persisting, or decaying intuitions as outcomes of assemblage		
Domains	P1: arranging understood activity	P2: assembled connections, patterns, rules	P3: facilitating altered understandings & preferences re interests & conflict	
Triadic Formats				
Format 1	Orchestrating threats to cut off a party's connections, arrangements, exchanges with others			
Format 2	Arranging 3rd party rewards & punishments			
Format 3	Receiving benefits from patrons or clients in return for brokerage			
Format 4	Arranging/maintaining separations between local group, periphery from center, or national from international actors			
Format 5	Arbitrating disputes; arranging negotiations, exchanges			
Format 6	The presence of marginal populations generates demand for brokerage			
Format 7	Limiting access to desirable arenas, conferring or withholding social status – thereby reducing client or customer options			

A few highlights and additional details. Broker power flows from access to resources (wealth, information, minerals), network positions, and their ability to resolve organizational CAPs for various constituencies. Power facilitates arranging and mediating patron–client, client–client, and patron–patron relationships, sometimes with reinforcing or undermining influence. When they empower disparate local groups by resolving CAPs of mobilization, brokers may also resolve the center's CAPs of extending authority – by maintaining inter-group divisions.

The often-subtle instruments of broker power include implied rewards and punishments related to assembling, disassembling, enhancing, or undermining relationships, exchanges, and manipulative narratives. Manifestations: temporary brokerage "fixes" exhibit de facto power. Longer-term impacts on the strength and sustainability of formal institutions confer de jure power.

Brokers utilize power's three domains. Organizing a militia assault constitutes power1. Powers 2 and 3 operate when brokerage uncovers or constructs previously unseen sanctions; it may bias information, communication, and understandings about the behavior and proclivities of others. Broker power2 includes facilitating new threats, altering agendas, and constructing barriers to access. Expectations change accordingly. Broker power3 emerges from assembling narratives that frame interpretations of social environments, including normative prescriptions, towards or away from local, regional, national, or international conflict. Such framing may promote stereotypes of other groups (dishonest, lazy). Broker activity can generate issues of contention or alter understandings of the "sides" in disputes, implied dangers, who to blame, and so forth.

In such endeavors, brokers utilize power's seven triadic formats. As they assemble, dismantle, or meddle in relationships and transactions, they ostracize enemies (F1) and recruit others to perform the "dirty work" of punishing undesirables (F2). They profit from taking sides in disputes (F3). They sow and maintain division among clients and between patrons and clients (F4). They mediate (F5). They profit from the presence of marginal parties (F6). As gatekeepers (F7), brokers limit entry into desirable economic, political, and social arenas – truncating choices for other participants, customers, and clients.

Broker power thereby shapes micro, meso, and macro institutional evolution. In Southeast Asia, "... the infrastructure of migration is by no means autonomous but is rather structured according to the uneven political, economic, and social systems that it traverses, thus often disturbing any easy distinctions between state and private actors. Brokers are located at the intersections of these actors and systems" (Lindquist, 2012, 319).

Macro-level impacts – especially in regions with contested rules and boundaries – follow from broker influence on bargaining processes and distributions of benefits that underlie political settlements (Goodhand and Walton, 2022). Such influence is often most pronounced within less cohesive, multipolar political settlements and during transitions between settlements. The punctuation of a prior social equilibrium invites brokerage.

Because brokers invest resources into these endeavors. They operate as institutional entrepreneurs – Section 4's topic.

4 Institutional Entrepreneurs

Institutional entrepreneurs "seek ways to do things which until now have been impossible. They cast around for elements of institutions that they could recombine in unusual ways at opportune moments in order to produce change"

(Crouch, 2005, 4).

Opposing claims to resources constitute the linchpin for the emergence of ethnocentrism or nationalistic sentiments about one's group. The group – ranging in scale from family to tribe to clan – develops a sense of kinship, fictive or otherwise, driven by the extent to which it is in competition with other groups over relative status

(Darity et al., 2017, 38).

Developmental dilemmas emerge from two interdependent realms of contestation: political-economic interests as they relate to exchange and authority; and social norms as they relate to social identities. Interactions in both realms invite and respond to conflicts over resources, position, political recognition, and symbols.

Building on Section 2's systematic approach to power and Section 3's discussion of leadership, following, and brokerage, this section considers a fourth, hybrid type of agency: institutional entrepreneurship. Section 1 discusses the basic concept. Section 2 discusses political-economic entrepreneurship, noting influences on conceptions of interests, positions of influence, exchanges, access, and participation. Section 3 discusses normative-identity entrepreneurship, noting influences in three areas: 1) the scope, intent, and strength of existing social norms; 2) the evolution of norms; 3) individual and group social identities. Norms and identities underlie understandings of social environments and, by extension, exercising agency. Section 4 contrasts multifaceted pluralistic social identities with narrow singular identities bound to ethnicity, race, and/or religion. Identity singularity fosters developmental dilemmas of social cleavage and inter-group conflict – such as the discordant legacy of the 1947 partition of India and Pakistan.

4.1 The Concept of Institutional Entrepreneurship

Business entrepreneurs invest money into developing new products and technologies – for profit. *Institutional entrepreneurs* (IEs) invest economic and political resources into reconfiguring informal and formal institutions, in pursuit of shifting political, economic, and social goals (DiMaggio, 1988; Crouch, 2005; Pachero et al., 2010; Battilana et al., 2014; Grillitsch and Sotaruta, 2020). They initiate and implement institutional change. Recall from Section 2: institutions are shared mental models that shape motivation, information flows, and cognitive framing of social environments. Accordingly, IEs arrange rewards and punishments, disperse and withhold information, and shape common understandings of pertinent social categories and relationships.

IEs are agents of collective action who discover, evaluate, and exploit opportunity – directly as leaders, or behind the scenes as brokers. They perceive openings, often problems with status quo arrangements. They possess organizational and communication skills. They solicit, influence, and arrange followers, including notable people, enforcers, organizations, and groups.

Leaders lobby, initiate procedural challenges, recruit oppositional coalitions, and organize armed groups. They orchestrate or disrupt procedures, rules, and platforms, as well as coalitions and alliances. They negotiate arrangements among competing parties. They bring together visible actors, who then influence their own followers, perhaps by forming political parties or militias. They block access to arenas and processes. They break barriers, violate norms, evade laws, and create avenues for response.

IEs also shape beliefs that underlie action and reaction. They broadcast shared mental models, via narratives and symbolic actions that frame or reframe common understandings of problems, procedures, and opportunities. They motivate and construct pathways for institutional change. They create legitimacy for new relationships or practices and undermine established social patterns. They reinterpret norms. They proselytize behavioral scripts that sometimes congeal into new norms. And they shape social identities, which incorporate, shape, and respond to norms. In so doing, they influence the salience of singular vis-à-vis plural identities, with calls to exclusionary ethnic unity or inter-ethnic cooperation. They enhance or diminish social cleavages, conflict, and social dilemmas.

IEs operate across scales, ranging from micro-level individual and intra-group interactions to regional policy domains and macro-level regimes and political settlements.

IE activity follows an evolutionary logic. IEs invest resources into discovering workable narratives and practices that operate as memes. A *meme* is a "combination of cues, narratives, symbols, or indeed any choice of communication" meant to alter political-economic practice, understandings, and social identities (Ash et al., 2024, 4). Meme propagation follows principles of reproductive selection (Dawkins, 1976).[38] People tend to adopt ostensibly successful ideas and actions; they eschew unsuccessful ones. Commonly adopted memes shape shared social understandings as well as social structures – configurations of roles, rules, and procedures wherein IEs, collaborators, and opponents exercise power and other forms of strategic agency. Who decides? What can they do? What are the issues of conflict?

These evolutionary dynamics mix four overlapping techniques (Pacheco et al., 2010; Sarasvathy, 2001, 2008; Lévi-Strauss, 1966; Gould and Vrba, 1982; Mokyr, 2000; Gould, 2002):

1. *Institutional adaptation*: rearranging patterns and procedures of coordination in response to changing circumstances. Section 3's discussion of the Wagner group mutiny illustrates Prigozhin's adaptive, yet ultimately unsuccessful, efforts at institutional entrepreneurship.
2. *Bricolage*: mixing or reassembling institutional patterns, relationships, and understandings – such as how norms of "fairness" relate to laws, regulations, and routine interactions within agencies, businesses, and constituencies (Cleaver, 2002). Ottoman sultan Mehmed II (1451–1481) restructured the empire's hierarchy and center-periphery relationships by incorporating Byzantine elites into ruling circles – rather than treating them as enemies (Barkley, 2008).
3. *Exaptation*: coopting the function of an existing technology or procedure away from its initial intent or unintended operation or role: " . . . a technique that was originally selected for one trait owes its latter success and survival to another trait which it happens to possess" (Mokyr, 2000, 87; Dew et al., 2004). South Africa's post-1994 land reform was meant to spread wealth to black constituencies and promote market mechanisms. Yet, IE brokers incorporated traditional elites, thereby extending the reach of ethnic hierarchies (James, 2011).[39]
4. *Effectuation*: trial-and-error utilization of pre-committed partners, recruits, and available means to address evolving goals – aiming to do so with affordable losses (Sarasvathy, 2001). Whereas traditional strategic logic posits *a priori* goals and selects means according to expected net benefits, effectuation entails on-the-spot adjustments of goals and procedures in

---

[38] Evolutionary game theory can illustrate.
[39] On political entrepreneurship during the post-1994 political transformation in South Africa, see Levy et al., 2021.

reaction to shifting uncertain contexts. Prigozhin utilized the given means of his pre-committed troops and changed tactics with circumstance. Reversing the Wagner Group's prior support of Putin's "special operation," he redirected its troops and arms against Russian army outposts. Responding to the increasing risks during their subsequent march to Moscow, he ordered a turnaround.

Accordingly, IEs "recombine elements, even fragments, of various governance forms that they find available, in an attempt to increase the range of capacities available to actors within fields of interest to them ... They might carry out costed searches into alternative paths... [or] transfer experience from different action spaces; or from other agents ... [They update] behaviour in order to respond to environmental path dependences." (Crouch, 2005, 22, 24, 86).

How do agents become successful IEs? Investments must reap returns. Prospects for success depend on projecting a vision for change and mobilizing sufficient support. Effective IE visions offer shared mental models that articulate the following elements (Battilana et al., 2014):

- Problems with status-quo arrangements, such as unfairness, exclusion, waste, corruption, and threats to group identity or survival
- A conception of preferred arrangements or a path to them
- A rationale that can motivate the effort of effecting change, such as material gain, better governance, or compatibility with prevalent norms or social identities.

A functional rationale for change must somehow coincide with perceived interests and notions of propriety or fairness and social identities of potential supporters. Prospects for success thus depend on the legitimacy of proposals and involved parties. Section 3's principles of leadership, following, and brokerage apply. Prototypical IE leaders, who share an identity with constituencies, face fewer barriers to recruiting supporters (followers) than non-prototypical leaders. IE brokers, who rely on recruiting others and arranging pathways, must still pay attention to the perceived legitimacy of recruited spokespeople and arranged procedures. Additionally, IE brokers utilize their network positions – local embeddedness, external connections, and/or liaison status – as they address demand for their services arising from external invitation, local quests for representation, or both.[40]

IE success also depends on meso-level field conditions, including spatial distributions of knowledge and services within relevant policy domains. These conditions shape opportunity sets, understandings, and relationships among

---

[40] Section 3.5 elaborates.

location-based constituents and opponents (Battilana et al., 2014; Grillitsch and Sotarauta, 2020).[41]

At both meso- and macro-levels, incongruity between informal and formal institutions marks a failure of formal institutions to fit social equilibria. IEs notice. Opportunity follows. At macro levels, IEs may broadcast or reinterpret ideologies as tools for motivating collective action and forging coalitions. They may influence the emergence or longevity of regimes and political settlements. Incoherent, multipolar political settlements – settlements that suffer from unresolved CAPs of allocating authority (see Appendix 1) – are particularly vulnerable to IE influence. Likewise, the unraveling of a political settlement – perhaps following conflict over social identities or resource access – opens multiple opportunities for reconfiguring political-economic rules and arenas.

All such activities rely on IE access to sources of power – resources, institutional positions, and abilities to resolve organizational CAPs.[42] They employ power's three domains and seven triadic formats. They combine power2 influence on rules and expectations with power3 influence on understandings of conflict. Such exercises configure arenas for direct, often confrontational exercises of power1 – often with recruited supporters or enforcers.

These activities operate in two overlapping realms of influence: political-economic entrepreneurship and normative-identity entrepreneurship.

4.2 Political-Economic Entrepreneurship

Political-economic entrepreneurship operates in two basic interacting fashions:

1. *Direct influence on interests*: Altering political-economic incentives by reconfiguring rules and associated expectations.
2. *Ideational influence*: Reconfiguring understandings and perceptions of rules and interests.

In economic arenas, direct influence operates on formal and informal exchange mechanisms, including types of markets, rules of entry and exit, contracting practices, enforcement procedures, and definitions of property rights. In the 1990s, small farmers in Peru's coastal agroindustrial region, Chincha, sold cotton without contracts to ginners who processed and sold it to textile

---

[41] Organizational fields are meso-level combinations of "key suppliers, resource and product consumers, regulatory agencies, and other organizations that produce similar services or products" DiMaggio (1983, 148).

[42] For Mukand and Rodrik (2018), *political entrepreneurship* operates in both domains. I prefer the breadth implied by *institutional entrepreneurship*. Related terms: *ethnic entrepreneurs* and *violence entrepreneurs*. *Public entrepreneurs* organize the production of collective goods (Ostrom and Ostrom, 1977).

companies. In contrast, large farmers sold directly to textile firms, using ginners only for processing. Following a decline in profitability, large farmers abandoned cotton to grow asparagus. One large farmer, however, as an IE, created a company that offered small farmers share-tenancy contracts and provided management and sales services for 25 percent of the profit. Small farmers became residual claimants to returns of their labor. Moreover, they contracted with ginners for processing and sold directly to textile firms. These innovative arrangements restructured local exchange relations (Escobal et al., 2000).

Property rights and enforcement mechanisms respond to political influence: who gets what, when, and how? (Laswell, 1936). Institutional economic entrepreneurship thus invokes politics.

IE direct political influence focuses on reallocating authority. Operating on the supply-side of politics, IEs invest resources into creating, altering, or replacing decision rules, rights, positions, and processes, related to *governance* – that is, the combined influence of governmental and non-governmental, official and unofficial parties on the allocation of authority and policymaking. IEs shift the bases of support and legitimacy of rule-making procedures, policies, and political figures. They are modern "princes" who utilize power strategically. They are resourceful agents who utilize cunning to achieve political goals (Dahl, 1961).

During the 1998–2003 rebellion against the DRC Kabila regime, entrepreneurial rebels established markets for protecting transnational traders on the Congo-Uganda border. These new institutions facilitated sharing the spoils of cross-border trade: "the gradual reinterpretation of existing regulatory frameworks – as well as the structure of social relations that underpinned them – fostered a transformation of the local institutional framework that defined and directed local political action" (Reymakers, 2010, 564).

Exercises of powers 1 and 2 impact interests directly. IEs alter incentives, expected reactions, and strategic calculations. IEs may bribe or lobby officials – power1. Utilizing power2, they influence who attends meetings, who speaks, who sets agendas, who competes for influential positions, and who votes. They threaten punishment for attending demonstrations, offering dissenting opinions in print or at meetings, or for testifying in court. They assemble coalitions.

Ideational influence utilizes power3. To reconfigure political-economic understandings, IEs invest resources into discovering and utilizing narratives, symbols, and actions that reorder assessments of environments, interests, allies, enemies, opportunities, and issues of conflict, such as "proper" ownership and entitlement they invoke cognitive shortcuts and biases to privilege their ideas in political arenas, often targeting subgroups. In societies with weak institutions and abundant point-source resources – societies vulnerable to a *resource curse* – IE narratives may rationalize privileged elite access and dominance of politics with stories of heritage and prosperity.

Ash, Mukand, and Rodrik (2024) elaborate on *ideational* entrepreneurship, noting that it links political-economic and normative-identity entrepreneurship. They posit two ideational realms of influence:

1. *Worldview politics* addresses understandings of political-economic contexts, processes, potential changes, and associated interests. For example, a supply-side worldview opines that government regulation and taxation impede the natural productivity of free markets. Policies that benefit the wealthy encourage private investment with "trickle down" gains to poorer individuals. More generally, ideational political memes bias signals received by private parties by introducing noise and by blocking "information received about the state of the world" (Ash et al., 2024, 48). Propaganda serves this purpose.

When worldview politics militates against ideas of class conflict, it prepares the groundwork for the second ideational realm:

2. *Identity politics* addresses understandings of group membership, loyalty, and normative behaviour. It alters conceptions of social identity.[43]

In both of these realms, areas of influence range from small-group ideas about production, exchange, value, politics, propriety, fairness, and identity to paradigmatic macro ideologies. Identity politics raises the next topic: normative-identity entrepreneurship.

4.3 Normative-Identity Entrepreneurship

Social norms and social identities coevolve with mutual interactive impact. Both become shared mental models that frame understandings of social contexts. I first consider norms.

Social norms are mutually understood, informally derived behavioral prescriptions with ethical content that apply to certain social groupings in specific circumstances. As shared mental models, norms assign social meanings, such as propriety, to specific rules and behaviors, with typically vaguely implied consequences for nonadherence. Norms thus shape the *expressive dimension* of behavior – that is, the signals conveyed by specific actions in specific

---

[43] Ash, Mukand, and Roderick (2024) and Mukand and Rodrik (2018) model worldview and identity politics. Benabou (2008) models how political parties and interest groups influence ideologies and distort beliefs about government-market relations. Glaeser (2005) investigates entrepreneurial hateful stories, which succeed when claims appear genuine and ulterior motives remain hidden.

contexts.[44] Normative prescriptions send signals that distinguish "good" from "bad" activity or character. (Appendix 2 develops an applicable Bayesian signaling game.) Norms point to often overlapping and conflicting social roles ascribed to gender, race, caste, ethnicity, class, age, family position, and so forth. Moreover, because understandings of interests rely on social roles and contexts, norms mediate goal-oriented behavior. Normative prescriptions generate justifications for or against certain activities. In some societies, it is not "appropriate" for women to own land.

Ultimately, norms choreograph social activity (Gintis, 2009). In so doing, they utilize three informal mechanisms of coordination and enforcement that hold norms in place (Burke and Young, 2009, 3):

i. *Strategic complementarity (pure coordination)*: Individuals benefit by matching strategies with others, such as arriving at meetings on schedule or driving on the correct side of the road.
ii. *Sanctions:* Individuals anticipate nonspecific negative sanctions for observed violations or praise for adherence. Such expectations motivate conformity. Some follow norms just to fit in, "falsifying" their preferences (Kuran, 1995).
iii. *Internalization*: Some adhere to norms out of personal conviction. Violation, even when unobservable, evokes guilt. Internalized norms shape social identities (Section 4.3 elaborates).

Social norms, moreover, influence the viability of formal institutions. Laws that infringe on norms often fail to alter behavior. They prescribe activity that does not correspond to social equilibria. In such cases, laws may operate only as words on paper (Basu, 2000).

Multiple avenues for IE influence follow. IEs not only alter common understandings of proper roles for specific groups in specific circumstances – and possible reactions – they also exploit status-quo fragilities by propagating ethical prescriptions that undermine extant procedures, regulations, and laws. When formal institutions lack legitimacy, IEs can utilize disjunctures with prevalent norms to mobilize opposition. They may then address CAPs of reforming or abolishing formal institutions. On a larger scale, IE activity may undermine institutional systems that rely on tentative allegiance purchased via coercion. Highlighting the disjuncture between authority and proclaimed ideology, Vaclav Havel and other leaders of the Civic Forum helped usher in the collapse of communism in the former Czechoslovakia.[45]

---

[44] From Section 3: institutions are shared mental models that shape cognition; norms are informal institutions. For Cass Sunstein (1996, 914), *norm entrepreneurs* strive to change "social attitudes of approval and disapproval, specifying what ought to be done and what ought not be done."

[45] de Mesquita (2010) models revolutionary entrepreneurship.

Yet, such a resolution often creates new CAPs from ensuing inequities, inefficiencies, externalities, and conflicts. Prospects for inclusive development may improve or diminish.

As they pursue normative entrepreneurship, IEs utilize two broad and related paths of influence: interpreting existing norms and shaping the evolution of norms. For simplicity, I discuss these separately.

4.3.1 Direct Influence on Existing Social Norms

Normative entrepreneurship operates on the social meanings conferred by social norms. As mutually understood behavioral prescriptions with ethical content, social norms issue statements using an institutional syntax (Crawford and Ostrom, 2005). Norms contain the following types of statements:

- A = Attributes: the type of individuals to whom a norm applies, such as adult members of a specific ethnic group, women, or contract employees.
- C = Conditions: the conditions under which the behavioral prescription applies, such as when addressing an elder or while attending a community meeting.[46]
- I = AIM (middle letter), i.e., intent: the prescribed behavior, such as "do not cut in line" or "respect your elders."
- D = Deontic: an ethical "should." One should contribute to community projects.

Accordingly, IEs can influence the scope, intent, and strength of established norms. *Scope* refers to the A- and C- statements, which jointly indicate to whom, when, and where a norm applies. The prescription "do not cut in line" does not apply to three-year-olds or when there is no queue. IEs influence common interpretations. Is the cutoff age six, nine, or twelve? IEs also influence a norm's *intent,* its prescribed behavior (the I-statement). Does "cutting" include joining a friend in the line? Might interpretations, perhaps subtly, depend on race, ethnicity, gender, or social class? Related IE maneuvers alter the "rules of the game" for joining lines by shaping expectations and anticipated reactions: power2.

More substantively, invoking power3, IEs can affect understandings and preferences related to conflicts over adherence vs. violation. Manipulating I-statements can shift anticipated axes of conflict. Suppose a norm prescribes "do not challenge" a leader's authority. Does "challenge" mean asking questions or

---

[46] The Crawford-Ostrom ADICO framework also contains O-statements (or else) about rule-based consequences, with designated enforcers. Ferguson (2013) distinguishes types of informal institutions using the ADICO syntax.

physical confrontation? Such interpretations influence notions of conflict between "loyal" community members and nonconformists or new entrants, such as migrants. Preferences towards association and possible retribution respond accordingly.

IE power3 also affects a norm's *strength*: its deontic (D-statement). How bad is a specific violation? Does it "deserve" dirty looks, verbal confrontation, or violence? Does unintended violation count? Furthermore, IEs influence corresponding degrees of norm internalization. Those who value a norm would experience guilt should they violate it for material gain – as well as shame from anticipated reactions of adherents. Additionally, norm internalizers experience anger towards violators, which may motivate retribution.

More formally, equation (4) illustrates the behavioral statement of a given norm Ψ:[47]

$$\Psi : h(A, C; N) \rightarrow D_N(I|A, C). \qquad (4)$$

Here, h is an information set: a shared mental model that frames relevant social context in terms of A- and C- statements and N members of the relevant group. These terms jointly specify Ψ's scope: it applies to certain members of N (via A), under specific circumstances (via C). Reflecting Ψ's strength, h implies deontic (D_N): members of N "should" undertake actions consistent with Ψ's intent (I), given A and C.

Anticipating such influence, agents adjust their strategies (s_i) in response to the arguments of (4). More precisely:

$$\begin{aligned} s_i &= s_i\big(h_i(A, C, N); D_N(A, C, I)\big) \\ &= s_i\big(N, s_{-i}, \eta_\Psi(\iota_n)\big); \beta(\eta_\Psi(\iota_n)); \iota_i; \xi_i\big(\iota_i, (1-\eta_\Psi)\big); g(\iota_i); \xi_\eta(\iota_n); \varsigma\big(\iota_i, \eta_\Psi(\iota_i, \iota_n)\big). \end{aligned} \qquad (5)$$

Agent i's strategy (s_i) depends on the following terms: group size (N); others' strategies (s_{-i}); the group proportion of adherents (η_Ψ), which responds to (average) group internalization (ι_n); and expected consequences. The consequences of adherence depend on three factors: (i) social approval from adherence (β), which depends on group adherence ($\beta(\eta_\Psi(\iota_n))$); (ii) individual internalization (ι_i); and (iii) i's anger at violators, which depends on internalization and the group proportion who violate Ψ: ($\xi_i(\iota_i, (1-\eta_\Psi))$). Consequences of violation include i's guilt, which depends on i's internalization $g(\iota_i)$; anger from adherents (ξ_η), which depends on (average) group internalization ($\xi_\eta(\iota_n)$); and shame (ς,) which depends on ι_i and η_Ψ ($\varsigma(\iota_i, \eta_\Psi(\iota_n))$). Appendix 3 offers a more detailed model.

---

[47] An analogous equation, with additional commentary, appears in Ferguson (2013).

Now consider the probability that agent i adheres to the norm Ψ ($\rho_{A\Psi\,i}$). The following relations apply:

a. Increases in η_Ψ, ι_i, ι_n, g, β, ς, and ξ_η increase ρ_{Ai}, ($\partial\rho_{Ai}/\partial(\cdot) > 0$)
b. Increases in N and ξ_i reduce ρ_{Ai}, ($\partial\rho_{Ai}/\partial(\cdot) < 0$).[48]

Note that internalization levels (ι_n and ι_i) generate compounded impact, since g, β, ξ, and ς respond positively to internalization.

An application: In South Sudan, Nuer prophets have "defined the moral boundaries" of acceptable violence, thereby conferring and withdrawing legitimacy to political leaders (Hutchinson and Pendle, 2015). In terms of equation (4), information set h represents the shared understandings the prophets convey. "Boundaries" appear in A- and C- statements that specify to whom and when the I-statement about using violence applies. The "moral" component of observing boundaries – the D-statement – affects internalization, along with ensuing guilt and expectations regarding praise for adherence as well as guilt, anger, and shame for violation (ι_i, ι_n, β, g, ξ, and ς in (5)). The prophets' impact on political legitimacy (their combined power 2 and 3) emerges from and reflects common acceptance and internalization of their normative prescriptions – arising, from their moral leadership.

Now consider an IE's problem of attracting adherence to a tentatively acceptable norm (Ψ_b). A relabeled Figure 4 (from Section 3) with logic from (4) and (5) can illustrate. Let curves O(Ψ) and D(Ψ) now represent adhere (follow), F(Ψ) and violate, V(Ψ) (see Appendix 4). The curves now depict the influence of proportional adherence (η_Ψ) on a marginal player's payoff (ω_i) from each of these two strategies. Abstracting from unequal power relationships and agent heterogeneity, assume all individuals have equal influence on η_Ψ and have homogeneous preferences over strategies F and V. The following comparative statics apply:

- Increases in β and reductions in ξ_i shift F(Ψ) upward, moving the tipping point η_Ψ^* left, closer to the origin: $\partial\eta_\Psi^*/\partial\beta < 0$; $\partial\eta_\Psi^*/\partial\xi_i > 0$.
- Increases in g, ξ_n, and ς shift V(Ψ) downward, moving η_Ψ^* left: $(\partial\cdot)/\partial(\cdot) < 0$.
- Increases in ι_i and ι_n augment terms β, g, ξ, and/or ς: $(\partial(\cdot)/\partial(\iota) > 0)$. F($\Psi$) shifts upward, V($\eta_\Psi$) downward; η_Ψ^* moves left: $\partial\eta_\Psi^*/\partial((\cdot)) < 0$.
- Increases in ι_n increase η_Ψ, *ceteris paribus* ($\partial(\eta_\Psi)/\partial(\iota_n) > 0$). F($\Psi$) rotates upward, V($\Psi$) downward; η_Ψ^* moves left: $\partial\eta_\Psi^*/\partial(\iota_n) < 0$.

Assuming available data, testable hypotheses on each of these partial derivatives can follow.

---

[48] Because experiencing anger is unpleasant, $(\partial\rho_{Ai}/\partial(\xi_i) < 0$. Caveat on point a.: if $\partial\xi_i/\partial(\iota_i.) > (\partial\beta/\partial(\iota_i.) + (\partial\varsigma,/\partial(\iota_i.))$, then $(\partial\rho_{Ai}/\partial(\iota_i.) < 0$.

In these cases, as η_Ψ^* moves closer to the origin, the critical mass of adherents needed to incentivize conformist following decreases – simplifying the IE's CAP of inducing broad acceptance of Ψ_b. IEs thus influence normative social meanings, expected material and social payoffs, and strategic responses. Strategies F and V display expressive behavior by signaling attitudes that may provoke responses.

Again, IEs exercise power2 to alter scope and intent (A-, C-, I-) statements and power3 regarding internalization and associated understandings of the axes, degrees, and consequences of normative conflict (I- and D- statements). They reinterpret boundaries between permitted and proscribed behavior and the ethical severity of violation.

More broadly, such IE-follower interactions shape the often discordant, normative interpretations of social roles ascribed to gender, ethnicity, race, religion, political orientation, nation, heritage, and region.[49] IEs may also alter interpretations of the normative visions conveyed by prevalent ideologies.[50] The spread of Hindu nationalist ideology accompanied Narendra Modi's ascent to power in India, reshaping its political landscape. Such paradigmatic ideas influence political-economic development.

In these various endeavors, IE normative influence invokes power's triadic formats. Nonconformists (heretics) may be excluded from political-economic arenas – ostracization (F1). Moral prescriptions can recruit enforcers (F2); help align a small coalition with a larger one that would otherwise lack a majority (F3); divide opponents (F4); mediate internal disputes (F5). The presence of adherents can enhance an IE's ability to evoke conformity among doubters (F6), and IE normative influence can limit entry to desired arenas (gatekeeping, F7). More broadly, by altering distributions of power, such activity can reinforce or destabilize regimes and political settlements. Revolutionaries propagate oppositional ideologies to recruit followers.

Finally, norm internalization shapes individual and group identities and, by extension, inter-group conflict. Sections 4.3.3 and 4.4 elaborate, but first 4.3.2 addresses normative evolution.

4.3.2 Institutional Entrepreneurs and the Evolution of Norms

Norms evolve. Some emerge, some adjust, some disappear. Equations (4) and (5), with time subscripts, could illustrate their time trajectories. IEs shape such evolutionary paths by altering various social meanings implied by ADIC

---

[49] Eric Ohlin Wright's (1978) concept of "contradictory class positions" reflects discordant social roles.
[50] For Piketty (2020), ideologies justify various kinds of inequality.

statements – such as *fair, responsible, worthy, loyal*, or *outcast*. Shared interpretations and responses thus coevolve.

New behavioral prescriptions gain traction with sufficient following. With prevalent disregard, extant norms lose influence. Acting as leaders or brokers, IEs provoke and facilitate such responses. The conformity logic of Figure 4 again applies.

IEs can exploit fragilities within institutional configurations – especially arrangements that rely on weakly internalized norms and, often, coercion. IEs publicize hidden discontent. They address CAPs of changing, abolishing, or introducing new norms or formal institutions. In 1917, as he launched the Bolshevik revolution, V.I. Lenin exploited the weakness of the short-lived Menshevik regime, lingering discontent with the prior Tzarist regime, and widespread opposition to Russia's involvement in the First World War – all of which discredited traditional norms of obedience and patriotism.

Here is a stylized sequence. To create new norms, IEs announce new ADIC prescriptions, claiming that adherence will signal worthy moral character. (Appendix 2's signaling game can illustrate.) To attract adherents, IE leaders openly display commitment by demonstrating "appropriate" behavior. Brokers prompt notable or influential figures to do the same. Sufficient following transforms previously inert behavioral prescriptions into notions of propriety, with expectations of response.

Newly proposed prescriptions compete with both alternative IE pronouncements and established norms. Potential adherents respond, with attention to the position and legitimacy of signalers – as in Section 3's prototypical leadership, supply and demand for brokerage, and Figure 4's dynamics of common adoption.

IEs must therefore assemble rough coalitions of adherents: political exercises. Successful IE narratives can lower the reputational, identity, and material costs of violating current norms – often reducing incentives for preference falsification. When adherence to a new prescription achieves a critical mass, public adherence becomes socially acceptable and expected.[51] The new ADIC prescription morphs into a new social norm, perhaps prompting a new form of preference falsification and new CAPs.

Overall, IEs can reconfigure common understandings of the scope (A- and C-statements), intent (I-statements), and ethical strength (D-statements) of existing social norms. Over time, they shape the evolution of norms by promoting new ethical prescriptions and discrediting extant ones. The corresponding social

---

[51] Rapid acceptance resembles a social network *information cascade*. Acemoglu and Jackson (2015) model how observable actions of key individuals (leaders) influence norm evolution.

meanings of strategies Adhere (F) and Violate (V) respond to conformity pressure, praise for adherence, anger, shame, and guilt for violation, and underlying internalization. In institutional systems wherein weak formal institutions rely on discordant norms, IE activity and response may foster the punctuation of political settlements that underlie social equilibria.

Social identities enter these dynamics.

4.3.3 Cognitive Foundations of Agency: Individual and Group Social Identities[52]

As IEs operate on normative social meanings, they influence individual and group social identities. *Individual social identities* are mental models that locate individuals in society. They are a form of human capital that offers cognitive foundations for navigating complex social environments. *Group social identities* are shared mental models that convey common understandings of identifiable groups in society. They spawn intra-group social norms and choreograph activity. Group identities operate as collective assets that transform ascriptive characteristics (e.g., skin phenotype, language, accent) and behaviors into socially constructed categories (race, gender, ethnicity) and social roles. Political-economic influence follows. As they operate on such social meanings, IEs exercise powers 2 and 3.

This section addresses individual and group social identities and relations between them. Section 4.4 follows by discussing singular as opposed to plural social identities, noting relationships to social cleavage and inter-group conflict.

As mental models, individual social identities frame understandings of self in relation to others. They shape perceptions of a person's relation to social categories, such as race, gender, and ethnicity; behavioral prescriptions, such as "respect your elders"; and causal relations, such as anticipated responses to insults. As such, they establish cognitive foundations for relating goals to action, and thus for agency.

Individual social identities are partially chosen and partially socially imposed. "Individuals construct their own identity, but ... [not] as they please; they do not construct it under circumstances chosen by themselves, but under circumstances encountered, given and transmitted from the past" (Darity et al., 2006, 290). Individuals shape their identities by navigating given social categories, norms, and partially chosen affiliations with groups – often with attention to resource conflict. Although individuals do not choose socially

---

[52] This section merges and extends ideas from Akerlof and Kranton (2000), Darity et al. (2017), Darity and Stewart (2006), Darity, Mason, and Stewart (2013), Davis (2015), Sambanis and Shayo (2013), and Shayo (2009).

constructed categories and norms, they possess some discretion over interpretations and responses – as in degrees of acceptance or rejection of gendered social roles or devotion to one's parents' religion.

Equation (6) illustrates:

$$I_i = I_i\Big((s_i, S_{-i}); I_{-i}(s_i, S_{-i}); \varepsilon_i, \varepsilon_{-i}; \tau_{Ji}(I_J); \Sigma\tau_{J-i}(I_J); \Omega_J; \Psi_{\Omega J}; \Lambda_{XY}\Big). \tag{6}$$

Individual identity (I_i) responds to the following: strategies of self and others (s_i, S_{-i}); others' identities (I_{-i}), which respond to their strategies; individual attributes (ε_k; e.g. skin phenotype; shyness); the strength of affiliations with group J (τ_{Ji}; let $J \in \{X, Y\}$, where τ_J depends on group identity (I_J); the unequally weighted sum of others' affiliations ($\Sigma\tau_{J-i}(I_J)$; $\tau \geq 0$); group social categories (Ω_J), group norms ($\Psi_{\Omega J}$); and inter-group resource conflict (Λ_{XY});[53]

Group social identities, as shared mental models, convey common conceptions of group attributes, roles, and proclivities. They arise from cumulative combinations of individual identity expressions and group affiliations, in which powerful agents and IEs play disproportionate roles.

Equation (7) illustrates.

$$I_J = \theta\Omega(\Psi, S_{kt-1}) + (1-\theta)\Sigma S_{kt}(I_{kt}). \tag{7}$$

Group social identity (I_J) arises from the weighted sum of influence from given social categories ($\theta\Omega$), which depend on norms and prior strategies of all (Ψ, S_{kt-1}), plus unequal influences from individual strategies, which depend on social identities ($\Sigma S_{kt}(I_{kt})$).

Individual and group social identities coevolve. Their interactions reflect three key dynamics: identity externalities, group identity affiliations, and inter-group resource conflict. I address these in order.

Identity externalities. People prefer activities that affirm their perceptions of who they are (Akerlof and Kranton, 2000). One person's activity can influence another's experience of identity. Actions that match a person's understanding of appropriate behavior enhance that person's sense of self. By contrast, identity-challenging activity engenders discomfort – such as that experienced by certain males following the entrance of a female worker on a traditionally all-male construction site. Analogous externalities, with broader impact, may accompany group activities, such as open expressions of lesbian-gay identity. Too often, such externalities evoke perceptions of zero-sum tradeoffs, social cleavage, and inter-group conflict. Fertile terrain for IE intervention.

---

[53] Skin phenotype (color) is exogenous, biological. Race is an endogenous, socially constructed interpretation of physical and cultural characteristics (Darity et al., 2013).

Group affiliations. Individual associations with groups are partially voluntary and partially socially imposed. In either case, affiliations shape social identities. Relevant groups include religions, ethnic groups, political coalitions, and even sports clubs. Because human satisfaction responds to invidious comparisons (Solnick and Hemenway, 1998; Veblen, 2005), group attachments spawn both within-group solidarity and inter-group conflict.

Within given historical/cultural contexts, the discretionary element of individual attachment to groups, say X or Y, responds to tradeoffs across three factors (Shayo, 2009; Sambanis and Shayo, 2013):

1. A material factor: the X–Y difference in anticipated net material benefits.
2. A *cognitive factor*: assessment of the social distance between an individual and the perceived prototypical members of X and Y.
3. An *affective factor*: a comparison of X vs. Y status, reflected in relative resource access.

Appendix 5 offers a model.

Resource conflict. The relative status of groups X and Y – hence their desirability – depends on the between-group distribution of political-economic resources. Pertinent resources include wealth, land, political positions, information, communication platforms, and point-source resources, such as minerals, diamonds, and oil.[54] Ensuing competition over distribution – often perceived as a zero-sum game – cultivates conflict that shapes social identities. "Categorical identity is deeply embedded in intergroup inequality relationships" (Davis, 2015). To enhance group status, members issue threats and seize land or positions – imposing externalities on rivals and enhancing the grip of group loyalty norms.

Returning to coevolution between individual and group social identities, consider the arguments of equations (6) and (7). Social categories (Ω), norms (Ψ), and the weight placed on cultural influence (θ) emerge from historical processes. They are quasi-parameters: exogenous in the short run but endogenous to identity coevolution over longer time horizons. Within social contexts, individual activity responds to identity externalities; material, cognitive, and affective affiliation tradeoffs; and resource conflict.

Jointly, (6) and (7) illustrate the following principles:

- Ω, Ψ, and group social identities (I_J) are shared mental models.
- Ω, Ψ, and others' strategies (S_{-i}) represent social influences on individual identity (I_i).

---

[54] "Competition over material resources lies at the heart of persistent group affiliation and attachment" (Darity et al., 2017, 38).

- s_i and S_{-i}, interacting with Ω, Ψ, I_J, and resource conflict (Λ_{XY}), generate identity externalities.
- Group affiliations (τ_{Jk}) combine social influence and individual choice, both of which respond to the other terms.
- s_i reflects individual i's agency.
- Λ_{XY} represents the influence of resource conflict on individual and group social identity.

Herein, the material, cognitive, and affective motives for group affiliation generate the following choice dynamics: Operating within given social constraints and for given perceived social distances and net benefits, individuals prefer affiliation with higher status groups. Given benefits and status, they prefer groups with less social distance from themselves. Given social distance and status, they prefer groups with higher net benefits. These interactions (reflected in equations (6), (7), and Appendix 5) engender a *social identity equilibrium* – a steady-state profile of behaviors and affiliations that exhibits three principles (Shayo, 2009, 147–152):

i. Individual behavior is consistent with social identity.
ii. Social identities are consistent with the broader social environment.
iii. The social environment is the outcome of combined individual behavior.

Identities are thus endogenous to social relationships. Group comparisons frame individual identity concepts: "people 'find' they possess certain social group identities" (Davis, 2015).[55]

Hence, on the one hand, individuals construct their identities around affiliations with groups, categories, norms, status, and inter-group conflict.[56] They assemble identities using "technology from the public stock of pre-existing cultural knowledge and modifications" (Darity and Stewart, 2006, 291). With limited discretion, they rank desired group affiliations using combined assessments of material, cognitive, and affective group factors. On the other hand, the production and expression of private identities creates identity externalities with public-good characteristics that infuse group identity dynamics. Within groups, positive identity externalities enhance solidarity, as in identity-affirming chants, songs, and hymns within political and religious groups.[57] *Group altruism* creates a willingness to sacrifice material payoff for group benefit (Bernard et al., 2006).

---

[55] Equations (7) and (8) represent substantively and boundedly rational responses to social context and activity and cumulative adaptive learning that shapes norms and social classifications.

[56] Davis (2015) asserts that groups, rather than individuals, are the fundamental unit of social analysis.

[57] An old American trade union song: "When the union inspiration through the workers' blood shall run/There can be no power greater anywhere beneath the sun/ ... Solidarity forever ..."

Exclusionary group altruism, often an outcome of parochial empathy and rivalry over status, evokes punishments for nonconformists, negative externalities for outsiders, and between-group hostility (Bruneau et al., 2017). Within Kenya's ethnic politics, "group altruism, combined with between group antagonisms, creates material incentives for the reproduction of ethnic identity norms." (Gĩthĩnji, 2015, 91).

Furthermore, groups with strong identity affiliations develop internal norms that prescribe appropriate member behavior, and internalized group norms shape individual identities. Group-specific norms – reflecting cultural history, affiliation, ascriptive characteristics, and distributional conflict – become collective property that guides group behavior. Ensuing group social identities, again as shared mental models, become club goods – collective human capital that translates ascriptive characteristics, such as skin phenotype, heritage, and language, into expected social, economic, and political roles. Race, for example, becomes a group asset, with "a wealth-generating characteristic... a racial identity formation process is strongly implicated in normalizing disparate economic outcomes" (Darity et al., 2006, 284).

Herein, group identity externalities often accompany perceived disjunctures between one group's norms and another's. One group's accent, dress, public statements, gestures, and selective altruism may conflict with another's conception of proper behavior. Resource competition magnifies these effects. Such disjuncture fosters social cleavages that underlie inter-group conflict, such as that between ethnic groups – yielding potent terrain for IE influence and developmental dilemmas.

Within these myriad interactions, two components of social identity condition proclivities towards cooperation and conflict (Brewer and Gardner, 1996; Thoits and Virshup, 1997; Davis, 2015):

- *Relational identities* are context- and interaction-specific. They emerge from role-based engagement with particular individuals in distinct social settings and associated networks. Within firms, for example, interactions among employees of different ethnicities and occupations shape relational identities. A person may identify with a set of tasks as well as idiosyncratic dealings with friendly or hostile colleagues, supervisors, and/or subordinates.
- *Categorical identities* abstract from such specifics. As social constructs, they emerge from classifications based on impersonal group attributes – such as skin phenotype for race and dress or language for ethnicity. They follow complex, often subtle, conceptual and strategic interactions across many parties – with unequal influence. Individuals, with occasional exceptions for IEs, rarely affect categorical identities, especially in large groups.

Relational and categorical identities interact. Comparisons and activities based on either affect the other. IEs may then promote social cleavage by enhancing the salience of distinct categorical identities. Xenophobia builds on narratives about incompatible group identities.

Acting as leaders and brokers and utilizing practices of adaptation, bricolage, exaptation, and effectuation, IEs influence social identities and behavioral responses – as they seek to alter institutional structures. Their exercises of identity politics frame common understandings of strategies, individual and group attributes, social categories, and norms – as well as material payoffs, group status, and potential resource conflict. By projecting narratives and symbols, IEs shape perceptions of skin phenotype, gender, language, and dress. They alter proclivities towards group altruism, group prejudice, and exclusivity. They construct or disassemble shared mental models that exacerbate or diminish the salience of identity externalities – such as imagined threats to one group's heritage or status posed by another's claim to territory. They influence group affiliations, with attention to perceived social distance and status. Resource conflict can reinforce exclusive group norms, exacerbate social cleavage, and precipitate cycles of escalating conflict. Recall, Section 3's reference to how Miloshevik's stories about the Ottoman Empire implied that Bosniaks threaten Serbia's identity and existence. Civil war followed.

By enhancing the salience of categorical as opposed to relational social identities, IE can displace inclusive social identities. Inclinations for conflict ensue, shaping vexing sets of developmental dilemmas. The next section elaborates.

4.4 Identity Singularity and Social Cleavages

Noting that identity is neither static nor one-dimensional, Amartya Sen (2006) asserts that singular – as opposed to plural – social identities foster social conflict and inter-group violence. One could model an evolutionary dynamic by adding time subscripts to equations (6) and (7). The singular vs. plural distinction merits further discussion.

Plural identities signify multifaceted understandings of self in various social contexts. A person may identify with religion, political ideology, ethnic group, race, occupation, marital status, age group, and preferred sport. Identity pluralism emphasizes the relational component of social identity: multifaceted self-understandings respond to different activities, encounters, and contexts that span social categories.[58] People of different races and ethnicities may work as colleagues; they may enjoy fishing or literature; they may share experiences as parents or teenagers. Intra- and inter-group cooperation follows.

---

[58] Davis (2015), citing Crenshaw (1989), uses the term *intersectionality*.

Yet, conflict fosters identity singularity. *Singular identities* elevate categorical differences above idiosyncratic personal attributes and relationships. Identity singularity offers a "descriptive misrepresentation of the universe of plural and diverse classifications that shape the world in which we actually live." Truncated self-concepts impose "excessive demands," yielding a "perceived absence of choice about our identities" (Sen, 2006). Accompanying group norms distinguish "good" from "bad" member behavior and invoke Section 3's principles of norm enforcement – coordination, sanctions, and internalization. The strongest devotees take the lead in sanctioning violators or, as brokers, prompt others to do so (triadic F2).

Identity singularity also reduces the salience of intra-group differences, such as many skewed opportunities conferred by unequal wealth and social class. Ensuing within-group altruism – for some, a genuine sentiment and for others a manifestation of conformity – prompts contributions to group club goods. Enhanced group capabilities may then augment economic, political, and social productivity. In Bosnia, for example, segregated schools receive larger contributions from ethnic groups than integrated schools (Alexander and Christina, 2011). The intensity of group altruism and means of support vary across groups. Expressions and impacts reflect the distribution of power.

More ominously, identity singularity fosters social division, encouraging violence (Ascher and Mirovitskaya, 2016). As shared mental models, singular identities rationalize degrading outsiders. Eschewing individual differences, insiders regard outsiders through "the illusion of a singular identity ... to be demeaned" (Sen, 2006, 8). Ethnic and racial stereotypes become endemic, cultivating social cleavages founded in group prejudice. "The material benefits associated with group identity affect the dominant group's attitudes toward and treatment of the out-group" (Darity et al., 2017, 40).

Group prejudice is not an individual sentiment. It is a manifestation of collective preoccupation with relative group position, embedded within contested hierarchical power dynamics. Consider interactions between privileged group A and outside group B. A's group prejudice towards B combines the following shared preconceptions (Blumer, 1958):

1. A's members are superior.
2. B's members are alien to members of A.
3. Group A has proprietary claims over land, finance, occupations, decision-making positions, and prestigious social positions.
4. B has designs on A's prerogatives.

Group prejudice invites and justifies social cleavage, inter-group conflict, and persistent between-group inequity – such as that posed by structural ethnic discrimination and structural racism. Prestige and racial/ethnic privilege are social resources. Exclusive club membership increases the probabilities of attaining various positions, such as CEO. Vicious cycles of conflict and singularity develop. The Russian invasion of Ukraine has solidified both Ukrainian and Russian national identities in a manner that legitimizes escalating conflict.[59]

Identity singularity explains why ethnic, religious, or racial coalitions often outperform class-based coalitions.

Furthermore, the presence of highly correlated social categories fosters an especially conflictual manifestation of singularity: *superfactions*. These arise when (Walter, 2023):

- Two distinct groups occupy adjacent territories, wherein each is prominent
- Group members interact "exclusively with their own kind"
- Each group's racial/ethnic identity coincides with a single religion and specific social class, reflecting unequal resource access.

Correlated social fault lines then amplify the divisiveness of between-group categorization. Predatory tribal agendas follow. War becomes "almost 12 times more likely than with more heterogenous groups." (ibid. 39).

For example, following Sri Lanka's independence in 1947, simmering conflict between highly educated Hindu Tamils, concentrated in the Northern Province, and the majority Buddhist Sinhalese, predominant elsewhere, erupted into the 1983–2009 civil war. Religious divisions deepened regional, ethnic, and class fault lines. Similarly, compounded ethnic, religious, and class cleavages in Rwanda, India, and the former Yugoslavia have also motivated violent conflict.

In such "identity marketplaces," ethnic entrepreneurs create and "sell" new identity categories to willing buyers (Sambanis and Shayo, 2013). Among others, Narendra Modi, Franjo Tudjman, and Slobodan Milosevic have marketed such compounded singularity. Developmental dilemmas follow. Ensuing ethnic conflict "destroys national resources" by undermining national identity (ibid. 296).

A simple model can illustrate. Begin with individual identity, emphasizing its dependence on group affiliation. Individual social identity, I_i, is a weighted average of categorical and relational components. Consider two weighted terms: one for ethnic/racial categorical identity (E) and another (Z) that combines other social classifications, relational components, and general characteristics, such as skill:

$$I_i = \lambda_i E_i + (1-\lambda_i)Z_i. \tag{8}$$

---

[59] www.washingtonpost.com/world/2022/08/24/ukrainian-identity-russian-invasion/.

Here, λ_i represents the salience of E: the singularity weight. As a variable, λ_i responds to social context, such as how visible ascriptive characteristics influence the social construction of E (e.g., colorism and race in the US, Darity et al., 2017). Broadly speaking, λ depends on the following: strategies of all (S_k); and social identities (I_k): the strength of group affiliations (τJ_k; social classifications (C_k), which depend on J_k and individual attributes (ε_k); pertinent social norms (Ψ_{CJ}); and resource conflict (Λ_{XY}), which depends on resource disparity ($R_X - R_Y$).

$$\lambda_i = \lambda_i\left(S_k, I_k; \tau J_k, C_k(J_k, \varepsilon_k), \Psi_{CJ}; \Lambda_{XY}(R_X - R_Y)\right). \tag{9}$$

Because individual and group social identities coevolve, group J's social identity reflects the collective relative importance that J's members and other relevant actors place on E vs. Z:

$$I_J = \Gamma_J E_J + (1 - \Gamma_J) Z_J. \tag{10}$$

Here, $J \in \{A, B\}$; A is the dominant group. Γ_J = group J's weight for E, denoting collective identity singularity – an unequally weighted sum of the λ_i. Accordingly, Γ_J responds to (9)'s arguments, with powerful agents having the largest influence.

To more clearly relate (10) to social context, consider this: Social cleavage emerges from reinforcing interactions between A's group prejudice and B's sense of relative deprivation, backwardness, and inferiority.[60] "For ethnic groups long subject to social humiliation, it may be quite understandable that dignity politics often trump good governance" (Bardhan, 2005, 123). Skewed distributions of income/wealth, human capital, and land aggravate B's anxiety over "backwardness" and A's group prejudice. Yet, claims to land, resources, and political recognition can reduce B's anxiety – adding social significance to their material desirability (Horowitz, 1985). Moreover, reflecting group prejudice, A interprets B's possession of or access to such assets as inappropriate and threatening.

Resource conflict thus emerges with perceptions of a zero-sum game – one that fosters and reinforces identity singularity. IEs then exacerbate singularity with symbols that reinforce both B's anxiety over "backwardness" and A's notions of privilege and prejudice.

This equation summarizes these relationships:

---

[60] I combine Horrowitz (1985) on ethnic conflict and "backwardness" with Darity et al. (2017) on resource conflict and group prejudice, and Sen (2006) on identity singularity.

$$\Gamma_J = \Gamma_J\Big((\Psi_J(C_j), \eta_{\Psi J}; \Lambda_{AB}(Y_A/Y_B, H_A/H_B, L_A/L_B, P_A/P_B); R_T(L); S_{A_B}(V_B)\Big). \tag{11}$$

Group singularity depends on group norms (Ψ_J, which depend on C_J), proportional norm adherence ($\eta_{\Psi J}$), and resource conflict (Λ_{AB}) and symbols favoring A over B (S_{AB}). Herein, Λ_{AB} responds to the following A/B ratios: Y = income or wealth; H = human capital; L = control over or access to land; P = representation in the polity. R_T = contestable resources, which depend on L. Symbols S_{AB} respond to V_B, the visibility of B's largely ascriptive attributes (skin phenotype, culturally specific dress, language). From group B's perspective, all partial derivatives are positive: each argument enhances Γ_B. Γ_A follows mirror-image logic; increases in these ratios rationalize group prejudice.

Equation (11)'s arguments illustrate Hale's (2008) assertion that understandings of ethnic identity provide "thick" social information. For Hale, *ethnic politics* concerns perceived interests, which operate through the conceptual lens of ethnic identities (shared mental models).

Now consider the emergence of social cleavage and potential CAPs of excess conflict. Echoing Sen (2006), I assume that the extent of A-B cleavage (Θ_{AB}) responds to combined group singularity (Γ_{AB}), with increasing returns. We have:

$$\Theta_{AB} = \Theta_{AB}(\Gamma_{AB}); \\ \partial \Theta_{AB}/\partial \Gamma_{AB} > 0, \text{ and } \partial^2 \Theta_{AB}/\partial^2 \Gamma_{AB} > 0. \tag{12}$$

Assume a disjuncture whereby Θ_{AB} increases slowly before the singularity tipping-point Γ^* (e.g., 0.75) and rapidly thereafter. Beyond a corresponding cleavage tipping point (Θ_{AB}^*), violent conflict becomes increasingly likely.

Suppose that groups A and B coexist peacefully in close proximity, without sharp social cleavage: $\Gamma_{AB} < 0.75$. Changes in equation (11)'s arguments determine whether they subsequently cross the conflict threshold Γ_{AB}^*. Several potentially testable hypotheses follow:

- Greater values of Y_A/Y_B, H_A/H_B, L_A/L_B, P_A/P_B, and/or S_{AB}, enhance sentiments of deprivation/backwardness and group prejudice.
- Greater sentiments of backwardness and group prejudice enhance identity singularity (Γ_{AB}).
- Greater values of contestable resources (R_T) enhance Γ_{AB}.
- Greater group norm adherence ($\eta_{\Psi J}$) increases Γ_{AB}.[61]
- Greater Γ_{AB} increases social cleavage (Θ_{AB}).
- Greater social cleavage enhances the likelihood of violent conflict.

---

[61] Relationships among V_B, Γ_B, and Γ_A could depend on S_{AB}.

To promote social cleavage, IEs draw attention to these distributional and symbolic factors.

Now consider an intermediate category of agent: *extremists* – those who strongly identify E and internalize singular group identity norms (Ψ_{JE}). Extremists may act as auxiliary entrepreneurs – leaders or brokers – who signal group loyalty by, say, harassing members of the other group. Such activity may reveal or exacerbate the vulnerability of extant pluralistic norms, leading to increases in singular norm adherence $\eta_{\Psi J}$ and, by extension, Γ_J and Θ_{AB}.[62]

To sum up, IEs operate as leaders and brokers who devote resources to discovering memes – symbols, narratives, actions – that could shape institutional evolution. To navigate uncertain, shifting social environments, they combine practices of adaptation, bricolage, exaptation, and effectuation. Exercising political-economic entrepreneurship, they exert direct influence on interests by reconfiguring rules of exchange, property rights, allocations of decision-making rights, and prescribed positions of authority. Utilizing ideational politics, they shape understandings of interests (worldview politics). Additionally, as normative-identity entrepreneurs, they reconfigure the social choreography of norms. They reinterpret a norm's scope – to whom and under what conditions it applies; its intent – the meaning of its behavioral prescription; and the strength of its implied ethical mandate. In so doing, they influence reactions to norm adherence and violation, including praise, anger, guilt, and shame. More deeply, IEs influence norm internalization – underlying senses of propriety. Moreover, to shape normative evolution, IEs challenge prescriptions that interfere with their agendas, often with open or orchestrated violation. And they demonstrate or arrange activities that signal their versions of proper behavior.

Furthermore, IEs manipulate the conceptual foundations of social agency rooted in various mental models conferred by individual and group social identities. Identities operate as individual or group assets that facilitate agency, by framing understandings of contextual and behavioral relationships to self or one's group. IEs affect dynamics of identity externalities, group affiliation, and inter-group resource conflict – as they mobilize expressions of social identity towards their ends. They influence the relative salience of broad pluralistic identities as opposed to singular heritage, racial, or ethnic identities – often by manipulating notions of resource conflict towards the zero-sum interpretations so often implied by identity singularity. Social cleavage and conflict follow.[63]

---

[62] Section 5 and Appendix 5 elaborate.

[63] Social cleavages can generate good outcomes. A combination of "political organization inherited from the pre-democratic period" and "the presence of a single, salient two-sided social cleavage" increases the likelihood of effective opposition to one-party rule (Tudor and Ziegfeld, 2019, 2).

5 Conflict, Power, Agency, and Developmental Dilemmas

> *From my own childhood memory of Hindu-Muslim riots in the 1940s, linked with the politics of partition, I recollect the speed with which the broad human beings of January were suddenly transformed into the ruthless Hindus and fierce Muslims of July'* (Sen, 2006).
>
> *"External attempts at reconciliation, such as the Addis Accord and the UN Operation in Somalia (UNOSOM), often exacerbated the situation due to a lack of understanding of the local power structures and dynamics. These efforts were marred by fragmented leadership, personal interests overriding national interests, and a failure to engage broadly with the Somali population."* (Hussein, 2025)

This Element opened with the following question: Why do well-intentioned developmental policies so often fail? Powerful agents – be they individuals or organizations – intervene. How then might a society create a sustainable path to inclusive political and economic development? More precisely:

1. How might they limit violence in areas with sharp social cleavages when powerful actors benefit from continued conflict?
2. How might they manage extractive resources to avoid a "resource curse" – especially in contexts with weak formal institutions?"
3. How might they address systemic corruption that so often attends dilemmas 1 and 2?

In the face of such dilemmas, how might a systemic approach to agency and power offer context-specific policy insight?

This section proceeds as follows. Section 5.1 extends Section 4's approach to institutional entrepreneurship, focusing on how IEs can utilize power to promote a rapid emergence of social cleavage and resource conflict. This emphasis offers insight into how agency and social context influence the emergence and tenacity of these dilemmas. Section 5.2 sketches an approach to unraveling developmental dilemmas. Section 5.3 then contrasts the developmental experiences in Somaliland with those of Somalia to illustrate how this Element's theoretical framework informs policy analysis. Section 5.4 concludes.

5.1 IEs, Social Cleavage, and Resource Conflict

Why did the partition of India and Pakistan explode into violence? How did civil war emerge in the former Yugoslavia? How did abundant cocoa production fuel civil war in Colombia? What has prompted continued ethnic resource conflict in the Democratic Republic of Congo? What social processes disrupt relatively peaceful inter-ethnic relations? Too often, institutional entrepreneurs (IEs) become catalysts and promoters. They seize opportunities to shape understandings of resource conflict as they promote explosive social cleavage. This section outlines this logic and sketches a model.

An extractable resource (R_T) lies within disputed subnational, regional, national, or transnational territory. Groups X and Y, either of which could be Section 4's dominant group A, both assert heritage claims to the surrounding land. The status quo, which relies on tenuous government authority, allows both groups access to R_T. Three types of agents – IEs, extremists, and other group members – might engage in fighting over R_T. *Fighting* includes demonstrations, strikes, and/or armed conflict. Three overlapping stages of escalation follow:

Stage 1: Enhance Social Cleavage

In period t_1, IEs from group-X invest in discovering memes to broadcast the "unfairness" of Y's access to R_T. Because the surrounding land has both material and symbolic heritage value, the memes attract attention. They propagate shared mental models that frame X-Y relations as a zero-sum land-resource conflict, yielding socially divisive judgments.

The associated narratives redefine:

i. Political-economic interests related to territory, wealth inequality, and position
ii. Norms of group loyalty and "true" group membership
iii. Group social identities, with bias towards singularity.

As exercises of powers 2 and 3, such memes condition strategic expectations and understandings of identity-cleavage conflict.

More specifically, IE memes reinterpret interests, boundaries of legitimate resource access, perceptions of other-group motives, terms of dispute, and the stakes involved. These memes promote shared mental models of zero-sum conflict. Heritage narratives decry Y's "trespass" on X's cherished territory: an identity externality. IEs reinterpret group loyalty norms (Ψ_X) to enhance suspicion of Ys and discourage interacting with them. Adjusted A-, C-, and I-statements might stipulate that "no adult should cooperate with Ys in business or social engagements." Stories of unfair intrusion invoke ethical understandings of resource conflict (D-statements).[64] Internalization of loyalty norms intensifies,

---

[64] As in Section 4.3, A-statements specify attributes of individuals to whom a norm applies; C-statements specify relevant conditions; I-statements specify the norm's intent; D-statements (deontic) convey a norm's ethical "should" (Crawford and Ostrom, 2005).

influencing proportionate adherence, group and individual internalization, and implying consequences for violation, including guilt, shame, and anger (respectively, $\eta_\Psi(\iota_n)$, ι_n, ι_i, $g(\iota_i)$, ς, and ξ_η from Section 4.3's equations (4) and (5)).

These actions and responses, including Section 3.2's leader-follower political dynamics of coercion, conformity, and evaluation, enhance identity singularity. Recall, group singularity (Γ_J in equation (10)) is an unequally weighted sum of individual identity singularity (λ_i in (8)). Weights reflect power. IE narratives influence individual and group identities by redefining group affiliations (τJ), social categories (C), group norms (Ψ_{CJ}), and resource conflict ($\Lambda_{XY}(R_X - R_Y)$). Identity externalities proliferate. Social cleavages (Θ from equation (12)) intensify.

At the end of t_1, these interactions have reconfigured the interest-based, normative, and identity underpinnings of social cleavage. Identity singularity among extremists approaches a tipping point, sowing the seeds for conflict in Steps 2 and 3.

Stage 2: Precipitate An Incident

At the onset of t_2, group-X entrepreneurs introduce additional memes – perhaps stories about how Y's treachery poses an existential threat to X's way of life (power3).[65] Extremist social identities rapidly become singular ($\Gamma_{EXTX} > \Gamma_{EXTX*}$). They develop their own extremist group norm (Ψ_{EXTX}): a call to action against Y. They sabotage a Y facility or attack a few unlucky or prominent Ys. Group-Y extremists respond. By intensifying perceptions of resource and identity conflict, the incidents undermine previous inter-group sympathy and nonconflictual X-Y interactions. At the end of t_2, extremist singularity begins to spill over to the populations of both groups.

Stage 3: Expand and Intensify Conflict[66]

At the onset of t_3, X and Y extremists emerge as secondary (or subsequent) IEs. They pronounce, demonstrate, or arrange the dissemination of conflict memes that frame t_2 incidents and responses as threats to group prosperity, social identity, and survival. Power3. Fear increases. Identity singularity intensifies. Extremist normative calls to action (Ψ_{EXTJ}) spread across populations. Within both groups, singularity crosses the tipping point for disruptive social cleavage ($\Gamma_{XY} > \Gamma^*_{XY} \to \Theta_{XY}$ in (12)). Confronting the other group becomes a social obligation. Average members consider fighting.[67]

---

[65] As in Section 2, power1: utilizes direct, observable, and understood applications of force or bargaining strength; power2 alters "rules of the game" and corresponding expectations; power3 alters understandings and preferences about conflict (Lukes, 1974).

[66] Note the parallel to the intensification of conflict in Schatschneider (1960).

[67] Note the analogy to the "edge of chaos" in complexity theory (Miller and Page, 2007).

In the transition to active fighting, stage-2 incidents motivate aggression via two pathways:

1. *Unraveling preference falsification*: At the outset of t_2, potential followers choose No Fight (Figure 4's Nash equilibrium rests at Obey; also see Appendix 4). Yet, some Xs privately prefer denying Y's access to R_T. Extremist incidents then reveal a willingness to risk fighting over R_T. Inhibitions regarding public expression of hostility diminish. Singularity increases. Assuming heterogeneous preferences about fighting (not shown in Figure 4), those most opposed to the status quo, follow extremists with open support and additional incidents, revealing additional opposition. Others catch on. Augmented public opposition enhances conformity pressure to fight, and anticipated costs diminish. If expected opposition crosses a tipping point (η_{fX}^*), average group members encounter mounting social pressure to fight. Conflict follows.
2. *Altered understandings of status-quo resilience*:[68] For any given level of public opposition (η_{fX}), stage-2 incidents imply status-quo vulnerability. Anticipated probabilities of successful fighting increase even if stage-2 incidents do not reveal private discontent – as in cases where broad opposition is common knowledge, but pessimism has deterred action. Now, Figure 4's Obey and Disobey ($O(\eta)$ and $D(\eta)$) curves shift inward, moving the tipping-point (η_{fX}^*) closer to the origin. This dynamic simplifies the associated CAPs of organizing opposition.

Johannesburg's 1976 uprising signaled an underlying weakness of South Africa's deeply unpopular apartheid regime.

During t_3, additional IE and extremist memes stress "proper" ownership of R_T and threats to group identity. Singularity and social cleavage (Γ_J in (10); Θ_{AB} in (12)) increase, lending additional legitimacy to escalating extremist incidents. Normative calls for action surge. Group members update their expectations about the costs of fighting and probabilities of success.[69] Each member decides whether to invest resources (time, energy) into fighting. Appendix 5 models the transition towards fighting (F) and the corresponding intensity of conflict (Ω_{XY}). Here is its concluding equation:

$$\Omega_{XY} = \Omega_{XY}(\Gamma_{XY}, \Theta_{XY}, F_X, F_Y). \tag{13}$$

Fighting and identity singularity reinforce each other as they enhance social cleavage (Θ_{XY}). Mounting social cleavages augment perceived material and

---

[68] de Mesquita (2010) applies this argument to revolutionary entrepreneurs.
[69] Bayesian models could elaborate.

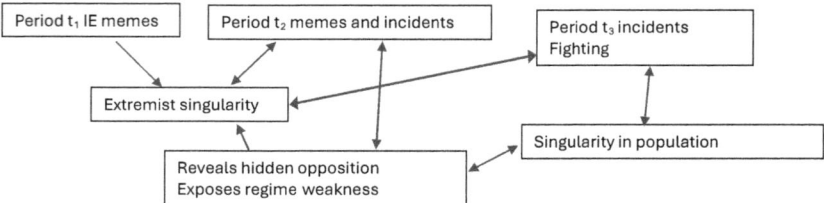

Figure 5 Singularity-conflict feedback

social incentives to fight. Within each group, proportion m_J ($0 \leq m_J \leq 1$) invests in fighting (F). Members of both groups engage in power1 conflict within newly formulated and understood arenas. The group with the greater F seizes R_T. Ensuing confrontations reinforce identity singularity and social cleavage with positive feedback. Figure 5 sketches the process.

With continued singularity-fighting feedback, conceptual and normative grounds for ethnic cleansing may develop. The onset of civil war in the former Yugoslavia illustrates the three stages of emerging conflict:

Stage 1: Following the death of President Josip Tito in 1980, ethnic tensions increased, exacerbated by subsequent economic decline. During the mid to late 1980s, Serbian communist-turned-nationalist leader Slobodan Milosevic became a normative-identity IE, stoking conflict between Serbs, Croats, Bosniaks, and ethnic Albanians. He "decided to make a name for himself by capitalizing on these ethnic divisions ... by emphasizing ethnic identity rather than political ideology" (Walter, 2023, 31). He promoted Serbian identity singularity (Γ_X) using narratives about Serbia's "cherished homeland." His 1989 speech on the 600th anniversary of the Battle of Kosovo, fought between Serbs and Ottomans, implied threats to the Serbian nation, notably from Bosniaks. By 1990, Croatian IE, Franjo Tudjman, used similar narratives to incite anti-Serb ethnic nationalism (Γ_Y). Fear spread, and social cleavages widened.

Stage 2: Serb militants attacked Croatian police units, and Croatian extremists responded. The incidents provided convenient evidence for Milosevic's and Tudjman's divisive claims. Coalitions of extremists coordinated and incited further conflict. Acrimonious rhetoric and action also targeted Bosniaks and ethnic Albanians, fostering incidents in Bosnia-Herzegovina and Kosovo. The previously peaceful multi-ethnic city, Sarajevo, erupted into conflict, initiating stage 3.

Stage 3: Steadily mounting rhetoric and incidents provoked escalating conflict that erupted into civil war in three theatres: Serbia vs. Croatia; Serbia vs. Bosnia-Herzegovina; Serbia vs. Kosovo. Even though many Serbs regarded Milosevic as a power-hungry opportunist, they acquiesced. They followed their prototypical leader-broker-IE. Perceived threats to social identity overcame prior hesitancy over his intentions. Barbara Walter, referring to Milosevic and Tudjman as *ethnic entrepreneurs*, concludes:

> Yugoslavia didn't erupt into civil war because Croats, Serbs, and Bosniaks had an innate primordial hatred for one another. It erupted because opportunistic leaders tapped into fears and resentments and then released small groups of well-armed thugs on the population in order to gain power (Walter, 2023, 38).

Again, powers 3, 2, and 1 permeate these interactions. Table 5 elaborates by relating the seven triadic formats to the stages of conflict, focusing on group-X IEs. Parallel logic applies to Ys.

Here are a few details. Recall from Section 2.2 that triadic power implies that a dominant party (A) exercises power over another (B), utilizing the actions or presence of third parties (C) as leverage – sometimes exercising power over C as well. During the pre-conflict period t_0, as they invest in discovering memes, IEs examine possible entrées for triadic formats. They investigate within- and between-group relationships that triadic power could affect – perhaps methods of and targets for ostracization, division, and mediation; or likely recruits for punishing adversaries. The seven triadic formats then apply to the three stages.

Regarding F1, stage-1 memes threaten disapproval or ostracization of Xs who interact with Ys. Public expression of pluralistic identities diminishes. Stage-2 memes and incidents enhance these threats, extending them to Ys who interact with Xs or who profit from R_T. Normal Y–Y interactions, such as community meetings, suffer, as do Y's relations with external authorities, foreign firms, and NGOs. Implied threats may also implicate external parties: NGOs beware. Stage 3 conflict amplifies threats via more dramatic ethical and existential implications of X–Y conflict.

Regarding F2, IE brokers recruit community leaders or notables (Cs) to invest in Stage-1 memes and subsequently to precipitate stage-2 incidents. IEs assemble methods and avenues for incidents. During stage 3, they recruit fighters and accomplices.

Regarding F3, during all three stages, IEs brokers seek rewards from external authorities, business interests, group Y dissidents, and group-X extremists for investing in memes, precipitating incidents, and recruiting fighters against Y.

Regarding F4, group-X entrepreneurs invest in stage-1, 2, and 3 memes that foster divisions within Y and between Y and external parties. Complementary narratives arouse resentment towards Xs who cooperate with Y. Stage-2 incidents physically illustrate and promote such divisions.

Table 5 Entrepreneurial triadic formats and stages of conflict

Format	Before Stage 1 (t_0)	Stage 1 (t_1)	Stage 2 (t_2)	Stage 3 (t_3)
Format 1: threaten interactions with 3rd parties; ostracize	Investigate vulnerabilities	IE memes imply threats to X's who interact with Y's	Incidents enhance stage −1 threats. Implicitly threaten Ys (Xs) who interact with Xs (Ys)	Threaten ostracization for Xs who do not fight
Format 2: use 3rd parties to punish	Investigate 3rd-party proclivities	Recruit community leaders to invest in memes	Locate extremists Forge core coalitions; Prompt incidents	Recruit fighters Arrange avenues for fighting
Format 3: seek reward for taking sides in 3rd party disputes	Investigate extremist-moderate and Y-external actor divisions	Payment for memes from Extremists or Dissident Ys External interests hostile to Y	Rewards for org. incidents from Other IEs, Extremists, External interests	Reward for Fighting from Extremists Dissident Ys External interests
Format 4: divide and rule	Investigate X-Y social cleavages, Factions within Y	IE memes sow division among cooperating X-Y members and hesitant Xs	Incidents enhance division. Moral narratives promote extremists.	Fighting divides remaining pluralists (hide or not?)
Format 5: Mediate	Internal divisions re importance of seizing R_T & threats posed by Y, esp. among potential extremists		Disputes within extremist core re type of incident	Normal member hesitancy

Format 6: Benefit from the mere presence of others	Investigate potential "threats" to R_T access and X identity threats posed by Y's presence	Memes: Y's presence threatens X's culture Y's proximity to R_T threatens "homeland"	Memes on Y's presence encourage incidents. The presence of Xs excluded from core (see F7) fosters core loyalty.	Presence of Y enhances X identity singularity & social cleavage
Format 7: Gatekeeping	Investigate desirable arenas	IE selects community leaders for "honor" of creating memes	Only most loyal allowed in extremist core	Form elite groups of fighters

Regarding F5, in all three stages, IE brokers arrange and referee negotiations over disputes among extremists, potential fighters, potential supporters, and potentially sympathetic external actors. IEs also facilitate implementing implicit or explicit agreements.

Regarding F6, suppose Section 2's parties A and B operate within group X. As pressure Bs to confront members of Y. Here, Ys constitute party C. An IE leader from X may disseminate stage-1 and 2 memes about how the presence of Y persons and customs threatens group X's social identity, access to R_T, prosperity, and even survival. Stage 2 incidents and Y reactions offer physical demonstrations of X–Y conflict, inviting intensified stage-3 memes. Brokers facilitate all such interactions. These exercises bolster the power of group-X IEs over hesitant followers and unify potential fighters – at the expense of internal dissidents and pluralists.

Regarding F7, a group-X IE (party Z in Section 2's Figure 2) limits access to desirable arenas, such as the "privileges" of issuing memes, joining the extremist core, precipitating or participating in incidents, and the honors of fighting. Exclusive access to such elite groupings bolsters loyalty among core extremists, as it reduces options for average members of X and coerces non-participants into acquiescence.

As illustrated by multiple incidents of ethnic violence and civil war, these exercises of power shape the environments within which developmental social dilemmas operate and evolve.

5.2 Unraveling Developmental Dilemmas

Recall Section 1's three interacting developmental dilemmas: (i) social cleavage/violence; (ii) avoiding a resource curse, whereby parties with substantial access to extractive resources or valuable agricultural exports dominate politics; and (iii) systemic corruption. As Section 1 illustrates, resource conflict and social cleavage reinforce each other. In societies with weak formal institutions, poorly defined and contested rights of access motivate material and symbolic conflict over contestable resources. Confrontations, sparked or stoked by IEs, enhance exclusive group affiliation, group prejudice, restrictive group norms, identity singularity, and social cleavage – generating more conflict. Corrupt allocations of access and benefits follow. Powerful agents direct resource rents to themselves, allies, and clients. As noted in Section 1, for over 100 years, transnational and domestic copper-belt elites have dominated Zambian politics, economic development, and the distribution of resource benefits (Bebbington et al., 2018).

These developmental dilemmas pose cumulative, reinforcing first- and second-order CAPs that create tenacious barriers to inclusive development. Powerful agents, as leaders, brokers, and IEs, gain by eschewing productive inter-group cooperation and exchange. Others go along. Micro-, meso-, and macro-level trade suffer, along with the provision of public goods, and positive exchange externalities. Truncated capabilities and understandings of methods of cooperation foreclose opportunities for myriad transactions, such as exchanging information, investing in physical and human capital, and advancing technology. Avenues for political access, participation, cooperation, and protection of basic rights remain underdeveloped. Widespread corruption, social cleavage, and resource conflict motivate systematic overuse of resources, constraining future revenue streams and undermining sustainability. Furthermore, second-order coordination and enforcement CAPs impede negotiating, much less implementing, arrangements for sustainable use, broader access, efficient production, and innovation. Herein, divisive IEs propagate stage 1–3 inflammatory memes and incidents, with zero-sum interpretations of incompatible interests buttressed by contentious norm-based singular identities. Conflict follows. Structural transformation fails. Limited access and corrupt distributions persist.

Unraveling these dynamics requires understanding them. After investigating the roots of developmental dilemmas, alternative IEs with pluralistic visions of inter-group cooperation should invest in discovering inclusive memes to unravel the cognitive grip of divisive memes. They should propagate messages of identity pluralism, with stories about cooperative inter-ethnic communities or workplace endeavors, or mutual enthusiasm for sports, music, and children. They might unravel zero-sum perceptions of identity and resource conflict by promoting positive-sum narratives about *communities of fate,* wherein members of groups share an understanding of interwoven common destiny based on mutual interaction. And members make investments in others' well-being. "People take responsibility for those in need, even if they are strangers or unlikely to be able to reciprocate." These interactions reflect a broad form of reciprocity that "implies community responsibility" and caregiving (Levi, 2025, 240, 241).[70]

As brokers, IEs could construct platforms for communicating inclusive memes and avenues for micro- and meso-level instances of cooperation. They might forge inclusive coalitions as they promote narratives, symbols, actions, and procedures to counter extremist incidents and discredit exclusive practices, norms, and corrupted institutions.

Disentangling oppressive webs of understandings and relationships that emerge from opportunistic exercises of power begins with relaxing the cognitive grip of power3-induced conceptions of conflict, such as the inappropriateness or futility of challenge. Then, altering power2 rules of engagement and corresponding

---

[70] On the economics of caregiving, see Folbre (2014, 2006).

expectations can, by reconstructing or creating arenas for interaction, prepare the ground for exercising power 1 to negotiate better outcomes (Gaventa, 1980).[71]

Economic development in the previously unproductive Greek wine sector illustrates the importance of addressing conceptual barriers, followed by adjusting rules of interaction, as foundations for constructive negotiation. To generate cooperation that underlay fruitful exchange arrangements, local producers, with some assistance from EU institutions, first unraveled cognitive obstacles to cooperation – such as mutual distrust and conceptions of futility. On this basis, local policies created "opportunities for deliberation among diverse stakeholders" to forge enforceable rules on cooperation, thereby resolving second-order CAPs. Credible negotiation about the terms of cooperation that facilitated market development followed (Gartzou-Katsouyanni, 2024).

More generally, to unravel developmental dilemmas of social cleavage, resource conflict, and corruption, pluralistic IEs must challenge shared mental models that underlie identity singularity, exclusive norms, and perceived incentives for conflict. They need to promote positive-sum narratives and compelling examples of cooperation. Here is a rough script:

- *Step 1*: Invest in discovering narratives, symbols, and actions that counteract the power3-grip of group prejudice and zero-sum understandings of conflict. Promote pluralistic social identities. Identify potential coalition partners. Stress the mutual benefits of cooperation with generalized reciprocity.
- *Step 2*: Demonstrate or arrange "incidents" of group negotiation and cooperation. Begin with small, manageable actions. Organize coalitions of dedicated pluralists as antidotes to extremists. Emerging informal and even tentative "rules" of inter-group interaction can then prompt expectations of cooperation among participants: power2.
- *Step 3*: Publicize stage-2 accomplishments, with a moral imperative to seek cooperation. Establish procedural and conceptual foundations for inclusive political and economic participation that render exercises of power1 by interests and authorities accountable to a broad public. Such actions generate new understandings of conflict and a new game (redirected power 3 and 2). Pluralistic groups may then negotiate (power1) more inclusive arrangements based on inclusive reciprocity.

Table 5's triadic formats, now adjusted to promote inclusiveness, apply. Pluralistic IEs should use Section 4.1's evolutionary practices of adaptation, bricolage, exaptation, and effectuation, with Section 3's principles of leader-follower politics and

---

[71] Unionizing one-company towns in early 20th century Appalachia relied first on promoting a vision of possible change (unraveling employer power3) before achieving union recognition (power2), which proceeded negotiation on the basis of bargaining strength (power1; Gaventa, 1980).

brokerage. Developing patterns of inclusive identity prototypicality can facilitate promoting cooperative norms and understandings of mutual interests, and plural identities: shared mental models of common community fate.

South Africa's struggle for liberation from Apartheid, illustrates.[72] *Step 1*: In 1953, as the leader of the Youth League of the SA National Congress, Nelson Mandela proclaimed: "Today, the whole country knows that their labors were not in vain, for a new spirit and new ideas have gripped our people." (Mandela, 1953, 21).[73] With this vision, a meme, Mandela sought to unravel Apartheid's power3-induced perception of invincibility. Coalition building followed. In addition to representing Black people across SA's tribes and homelands, the ANC recruited Indians and some sympathetic Whites. In 1952, the ANC and SA Indian Congress jointly launched the Campaign for the Defiance of Unjust Laws, which advocated boycotts, strikes, and civil disobedience – step 2 incidents. The ANC collaborated with grassroots organizations, such as the United Democratic Front (UDF) and the Congress of South African Trade Unions (COSATU). Large-scale strikes and protests, including the May 1961 general strike, called by the African National Action Council, the worker-initiated 1973 Durban Strikes, and the 1976 Soweto Uprising, demonstrated the breadth of opposition and began to suggest apartheid's weakness. The regime's invincible image, its power3, began to falter – as did the functioning of its repressive institutions, its power2. *Step 3*: Continued incidents, memes, and coalition building altered the rules of the game: power2 oriented towards regime change. Subsequently, negotiations with the de Klerk government (power1) established procedures for transition (power2), generating a new political settlement that underlay a new institutional system.

5.3 Developmental Policy Inquiry

Whereas specific policy proposals lie beyond the purview of this Element, its framework offers a foundation for developmental policy inquiry that extends beyond traditional approaches. How might societies and regions develop committed and capable governance that can deliver inclusive development? How might societies address foundational developmental dilemmas, including limiting social cleavage and violence, managing extractive resources, and addressing corruption without unduly undermining stability?

As policymakers and analysts endeavor to foresee the consequences of specific measures within specific social contexts, they should pay attention to principles of power and agency. Table 6 lists nine basic avenues for inquiry.[74]

---

[72] The actual timing of *steps* 1–3 overlapped. [73] Also see Mandela (1965, 1986,1994).
[74] Not meant to be a comprehensive list.

Table 6 Nine areas for context-specific policy analysis of developmental dilemmas

Basic Areas	Issues/Questions	Details	Details
1. First-order CAPs: Public goods Externalities Common resources	Barriers Opportunities foreclosed	Free-riding incentives	Underlying conflicts of interest & perceptions
2. Second-order CAPs: Coordination Enforcement	Obstacles to first-order agreement Implementation	Interests/understandings of powerful actors	Social cleavages
3. Power	≠ distribution: to whom? Foundation of PS	Sources Instruments Domains De facto & de jure	7 Triadic Formats Rel. to Resources, institutional evolution, Status-quo disruption
4. Institutions Formal Informal social norms	Social choreography Formal-informal compatibility Relation to social equilibria Power relations	Legitimacy Norm internalization Inter-group norm compatibility Avenues for IE intervention Relation to CAPs	Dist. of benefits to parties with disruptive potential Syntax (ADIC) Functionality of rules
5. Social Identities Individual Group	Plural Singular	Externalities Group affiliations Resource Conflict	Rel. to norms Social cleavages CAPs, conflict

6. Agency Individuals Organizations Coalitions	Leaders (L) Followers (F) Brokers IEs	Positions Goals/motivations Interests Understandings Power Rel to norms, identities	IE, L, & F political dynamic Prototypicality Conformity Coercion, cooptation
7. Ideas/Memes Narratives Symbols Actions	Political-economic Normative-Identity	Levels: Paradigmatic Problem definitions Policy	Adaptation Bricolage Exaptation Effectuation
8. Policy Domains	Region/issue Relation to Meso- power PS	Barriers, CAPs Pockets of effectiveness Ordered deals	Interests Understandings
9. Political Settlements (PS)	Typology Configuration of Political power: coherence Social foundation: breadth	Relations to: Institutions Policy domains Distribution Stability Paradigmatic ideas CAPs	Insiders/excluded Cooptation/coercion Legitimacy Dist. of rents to powerful

For each avenue, analysts should consider definitions, components, underlying logic, related concepts, and relationships to the other eight areas.

For each area, analysts should investigate possible openings, coalitions, concepts of interests, normative and identity frameworks that could motivate inclusive development, and relationships with the other eight areas. Multiple avenues for systematic policy analysis ensue. The developmental contrast between Somaliland and Somalia illustrates.

5.3.1 Somaliland and Somalia

In 1991, following a decade of civil war, rebels overthrew Somalia's Siad Barre dictatorship. In 1993, Somaliland attained autonomous rule. Depending on interpretation, Somaliland is either an independent nation or a self-governing region of Somalia. Its relative success in achieving peaceful settlement, political inclusion, and economic development contrasts with Somalia's experience of unresolved conflict and stagnation. A brief comparison illustrates this Element's principles of developmental dilemmas, power, and agency.[75]

Somaliland's developmental transition initially relied on locally led peaceful reconciliation, with representation across multiple clans. Ensuing stability facilitated inclusive locally initiated negotiation over governance, which responded to visionary, legitimate leadership. In 2001, Somaliland transitioned from clan-led joint governance to formal democracy, along with some economic development. By contrast, in Somalia, externally sponsored conferences gathered warlords, who lacked local legitimacy. The involved parties focused on state-building before addressing underlying conflicts. They strived to import external conceptions of institutions (i.e., "best practices") rather than foster difficult negotiation among fragmented local stakeholders. They failed to resolve second-order CAPs of coordinating and enforcing an end to conflict.

Tables 7A and 7B sketch key points of contrast and related analytical principles.

A few additional points. Somaliland's 1993 Borama conference, as part of a series of conferences, established the parameters of an emerging social contract. Prior conferences that focused on peaceful reconciliation established enough stability to facilitate negotiations on state-building and continued reconciliation. The Borama conference enacted the Somaliland Communities Security and Peace Charter, requiring local communities to control internal bandits, disband militias, and refrain from attacking other communities. It ratified the National Charter, with proportional representation that lent legitimacy to emerging formal

---

[75] This section draws on Hussein (2024). See also Bradbury (2008), Phillips (2013), and Menkhaus (2018).

Table 7A Developmental contrast between Somaliland and Somalia

Characteristic	Somaliland	Somalia	Development Principles
Background:[76] Coalitions involved in the overthrow	SNM: founded in 1981 Collaboration with local leaders, businesses, supportive diaspora, and clan elders (Guurti)	USC formed in 1989. Little collaboration.	Coalition building Inclusion of local clans & stakeholders Coherence
Political Settlement	Achieved coherent config. of political power & broad SF Disarmed militias	Fragile to nonexistent Incoherent config. of power Narrow SF with external influence No checks on power of warlords	Logic and types of political settlements Implications on institutional development & CAPs
Negotiation	Locally organized 1993 Borama Conference of Guurti: Included women Early focus on reconciliation Frameworks for security, governance & transition to civilian leadership	International sponsors Convened warlords who lacked local legitimacy No low-cost system conflict resolution	Importance of IE brokerage and leadership Local shareholder inclusion Constructive mediation (triadic F5)

[76] Different colonial legacies: Somaliland under British indirect rule and Somalia under Italian suppression of local institutions.

Table 7A (cont.)

Characteristic	Somaliland	Somalia	Development Principles
Social Cleavages	Diminishing due to cross-clan representation	Warlords stoked singular clan identities based on group affiliation and resource conflict	IE activity, norms, plural vs. singular identities, group affiliation, social cleavage, resource conflict
Social Contract	Transitional National Charter: 3 branches of government Proportionate clan representation Dist. of rents across SF stabilized PS & aligned business interests with long-term growth System of low-cost conflict resolution Transcended narrow clan interests	No comprehensive social contract No significant deals on rent sharing Few ordered deals	Constructive institutional entrepreneurship via leadership & brokerage Rent distribution ↔ support for PS Coalition building Cross-group representation Paradigmatic ideas of governance Some limit on power of local leaders can avoid the Acemoglu & Robinson (2018) civil society "cage" (Section 1)

Legend: Dist. = distribution; PS = political settlement; COPP= configuration of political power; SF = social foundation of PS; SL = Somaliland; SNM = Somali National Movement (operated in Somaliland); USC = United Somali Congress (operated in Somalia);

Table 7B Developmental contrast between Somaliland and Somalia continued

Characteristic	Somaliland	Somalia	Development Principles
Institutional Entrepreneurship, Leadership, Brokerage, Following	Visionary IE. Religious leaders (brokers) organized Boroma Conference which elected Egal 2nd president Paradigmatic vision Understanding of clans Leading role in devt bargain Centralized, managed patronage Disarmed militias, offered work in security services.	Factional struggles Opportunistic warlords No unifying leaders No common vision	Paradigmatic ideas of governance Leadership Brokerage Politics of leadership-following Adaptation, bricolage, exaptation, effectuation
Local vs. External Influence	Locally organized & funded conferences Major role for Guuarti, but Egal limited their influence External assistance for removing mines & demobilization of militias	External org of warlord meetings Focus: state building *before* reconciliation Ethiopia, Keya, and Egypt supported different warlord factions Some positive contributions: UN limited starvation & achieved some dialogue across factions	Importance of inclusiveness of PS Balance of participation Local initiative Stakeholder involvement and negotiation

Table 7B (cont.)

Characteristic	Somaliland	Somalia	Development Principles
Uses of power	Sources: Guuarti positions Coherent coalition resolved CAPs Power1: opposition to regime; assembling coalition Power 2: Rules for governance & reconciliation Power 3: Devt. vision reduced social cleavages Manifestation: both de facto and de jure	Sources: militia org. & arms Power1: Opposition to regime Warlord militia activity External funding Power2: Militia control local rules Warlords: Triadic F4, divided local populations External influence conference rules Power3: perception that militias provide security Manifestation: de facto	Relevance of systematic analysis of power importance of elements of power (Table 1) Importance of triadic exercises and formats – especially re externalities and subtle influence; role of brokers

Legend: Dist. = distribution; PS = political settlement; COPP= configuration of political power; SF = social foundation of PS; SL = Somaliland; SNM = Somali National Movement (operated in Somaliland); USC = United Somali Congress (operated in Somalia) institutions. The Charter combined local clan and Western conceptions of governance. These provisions facilitated business commitment to long-term development. Somaliland's second president, Mohamad Haji Ibrahim Egal, earned legitimacy by dismissing a member of his own clan from the post of port director. Egal's enterprising vision, leadership, and brokerage exhibited adaptive effectuation in his responses to Somaliland's CAPs and remaining conflicts.

Significant challenges remained: A conflict with the Garhajis clan, which felt excluded from prior agreements, erupted into violent conflict over the Haregesia airport – a resource. The combination of Guuarti mediation and Egal's leadership, utilizing both negotiation and force, resolved the conflict at the 1997 Hargeisa conference. This process illustrated the coherence of the Somaliland political settlement's configuration of power, with a corresponding ability to resolve leadership CAPs.

Overall, Somaliland's relatively inclusive and coherent political settlement and visionary leadership facilitated sufficient legitimacy for reconciliation and state-building that combined bottom-up participation with top-down coordination. Provision of services and infrastructure followed. Distributions of benefits involved returning land to war-displaced families, including members of non-dominant clans. Although its economy remains vulnerable to external shocks, Somaliland achieved some structural transformation in telecommunications and small-scale industry. In 2001, following a constitutional referendum, Somaliland formally transitioned to a multi-party democracy: a peaceful shift in the political settlement from traditional power sharing to formal democratic participation.[77]

Somalia, by contrast, failed to resolve civil conflict or achieve political-economic development. Continuing civil war after 1991 destroyed any preexisting state apparatus. Warlords exploited inter-clan divisions (triadic F4) by promoting singular group identities based on clan affiliation and resource conflict (power3). Substantial external influence, from the UN, the African Union, Gulf States, and (early on) the US, focused on importing formal state institutions before addressing underlying CAPs of social cleavage and violent ethnic conflict. The externally sponsored Addis Accord of March 1993 reflected a "top-down" approach without meaningful local stakeholder participation. Subsequently, fifteen participating warlords violated the agreement because it failed to address their interests in maintaining power. The Accord was incompatible with Somalia's social equilibrium. Moreover, the presence of foreign troops, culminating in the disastrous 1993 battle of Mogadishu (of *Black Hawk*

---

[77] Current transnational resource conflict over Red Sea ports may, however, threaten Somaliland's accomplishments and independence. www.economist.com/middle-east-and-africa/2025/04/16/a-new-smash-and-grab-for-red-sea-ports.

Down notoriety), further undermined the legitimacy of external intervention.[78] Although UN and NGO foreign aid reduced food insecurity and provided health services, it also encouraged dependence and even conflict. This provision reduced incentives to construct local service networks. Worse, it incentivized resource conflicts among ethnic elites over corrupt distributions. Somalia thus suffered from unresolved CAPs of social cleavage and conflict, a chaotic configuration of political power that precluded functional political settlement. No social contract ensued. "The result was a state of perpetual conflict, where the absence of a development agenda further deepened the divisions within society." (Hussein, 130).

A few policy lessons: First, address CAPs of excess conflict and deep social cleavage. Then, integrate continued peaceful reconciliation and state-building. Develop legitimacy by involving local stakeholders in negotiations and institution building, with attention to local governance mechanisms, combined with mitigating ethnic and regional social cleavages via broad representation. Balance centralization – as in coordination across clans – with decentralization via local participation (Hussein, 2025).

5.4 Conclusion

Again, why do well-intentioned developmental policies so often fail? Self-interested action by powerful agents intervenes. Achieving inclusive political-economic development entails resolving foundational collective-action problems – especially second-order problems of arranging coordination and enforcement of agreements that could, in principle, resolve myriad variants of first-order free-riding. Resolution requires crafting functional mixes of informal and formal institutions. Yet, powerful agents, pursuing their own agendas, shape institutional evolution because they can. Others follow or acquiesce. A foundational developmental dilemma. Corresponding dilemmas include violent conflicts motivated by deep social cleavages, avoiding a resource curse, and addressing corruption.

This Element outlines a conceptual framework for probing basic contours of political-economic development: a lens for policy analysis. My approach merges diverse components of the political economy literature. It builds on a systematic discussion of the thorny concept of power. Core elements of power include its sources, instruments, domains of exercise, and de facto or de jure manifestations. Seven formats – strategic templates – shape exercises of

---

[78] The abrupt 1993 US withdrawal and 1995 UNOSOM withdrawals may have exacerbated the problems.

triadic power – that is, power with at least three poles of interaction. This approach facilitates analysis of subtle power asymmetry and externalities involving third parties.

Four types of agency – leadership, following, brokerage, and institutional entrepreneurship – influence trajectories of developmental dilemmas via impacts on policy domains, institutional systems, and political settlements. Leader-follower interactions entail political dynamics conditioned by leader *prototypicality* – identity congruence with potential followers – as well as pressure from coercion, cooptation, and conformity. Brokers arrange interactions. As network specialists who bridge geographic, political, economic, social, and knowledge gaps, they forge connections, mediate, and limit access to desirable arenas. They shape the mobilization of power.

Institutional entrepreneurs (IEs) mix leadership and brokerage. They devote resources to transforming institutions. They invest in memes – narratives, symbols, and actions that influence common understandings, strategies, and behavior. An evolutionary dynamic follows. People imitate apparently good ideas and practices and discard apparently useless ones.

IEs operate in two overlapping realms of activity. Political-economic entrepreneurship entails altering incentives as well as ideas that shape understandings of interests and avenues for cooperation or conflict. Normative-identity entrepreneurship seeks influence over interpretations, impact, and trajectories of social norms – notably, their intent, scope, strength, internalization, and evolution. At a deeper level, IEs influence the cognitive foundations of agency conveyed by individual and group social identities. As largely shared mental models that frame understandings of individual and group social positions and roles, identities motivate both cooperation and conflict. Pluralistic identities encourage pro-social behavior, whereas singular identities engender the zero-sum dynamics of social cleavage and conflict.

Power infuses these dynamics. IE influence on *rules of the game* via norms and formal institutions, reflects power2. IEs also condition understandings of political-economic interests, normative prescriptions, norm internalization, and social identities – all related to numerous axes of conflict: power3. The seven triadic formats apply – notably F1 (ostracize), F2 (recruit enforcers), F4 (divide and rule), F5 (mediate), and F7 (gatekeep).

Policymakers beware. Prospects for policy success depend on specific social contexts shaped by these dynamics. At a macro level, developmental prospects reflect configurations of power and social foundations of inclusion and exclusion that underpin national or regional political settlements. Meso-level prospects reflect interactions within area- and issue-specific policy domains, such as education within provinces or cities- with attention to corresponding distributions of power and forms of agency. Inclusive developmental policy analysis and design should pay close attention to these dynamics, underlying principles, and implications on context-specific developmental dilemmas.

References

Acemoglu, D. and J. Robinson (2012) *Why Nations Fail: The Origins of Power, Prosperity, and Poverty*. New York: Crown Business.

(2018) *The Narrow Corridor: States, Societies, and the Fate of Liberty*. London: Penguin Randon House.

Acemoglu, D. and M. Jackson (2015) 'History Expectations and Leadership in the Evolution of Social Norms.' *Review of Economic Studies* 82: 423–456. https://doi.org/10.1093/restud/rdu039.

Acemoglu, D., S. Johnson, and J. Robinson (2005) 'Institutions as a Fundamental Cause of Long-Run Growth.' Chapter 6 of *Handbook of Economic Growth* 1(A): 385–472.

Afrizal and W. Berenschot (2020) 'Resolving Land Conflicts in Indonesia.' Review Essay, *Bijdragen tot de taal-, land- en volkenkunde* 176(2020): 561–574.

Akerlof, G. A. and R. Kranton (2000) 'Economics and Identity.' *Quarterly Journal of Economics* 115(3): 715–752. https://doi.org/10.1162/003355300554881.

Alexander, M. and F. Christina (2011) 'Context Modularity of Human Altruism.' *Science* 334(6061): 1392–1394.

Allen, T. (2015) 'Vigilantes, Witches and Vampires: How Moral Populism Shapes Social Accountability in Northern Uganda. *International Journal on Minority and Group Rights*, 22(3): 360–386. https://doi.org/10.1163/15718 115–02203004.

Anwar, N. (2013) 'Urban Transformations: Brokers, Collaborative Governance and Community Building in Karachi's Periphery.' *South Asian History and Culture*. 75–92, https://doi.org/10.1080/19472498.2013.863011.

Aoki, M. (2001) *Toward a Comparative Institutional Analysis*. Boston, MA: MIT Press. https://doi.org/10.1007/978-981-13-2757-5_25.

Ascher and Mirovitskaya (2016) *Development Strategies and Inter-Group Violence: Insights on Conflict-Sensitive Development*. New York: Palgrave Macmillan.

Ash, M. and D. Rodrik (2024) 'Economic Interests, Worldviews, and Identities: Theory and Evidence on Ideational Politics.' https://tinyurl.com/yb9u68zk.

Auerbach, A. M. and T. Thachil (2018) 'How Clients Select Brokers: Competition and Choice in India's Slums.' *American Political Science Review* 112(4): 775–791. https://doi.org/10.1017/S000305541800028X.

Bachrach, P. and M. S. Baratz (1962) 'Two Faces of Power.' *American Political Science Review* 56: 947–952.

Bailey, F. G. (1969) *Stratagems and Spoils: A Social Anthropology of Politics*. Oxford: Blackwell.

(2005) *Scarcity, Conflicts, and Cooperation: Essays in the Political and Institutional Economics of Development*. Cambridge, MA: MIT Press.

Bardhan, P. (2018) 'Reflections on Corruption in the Context of Political and Economic Liberalization.' Basu and Cordella, Institutions, Governance, and the Control of Corruption, IEA Conference volume 157.

and D. Mookherjee (2018) 'A Theory of Clientelistic Politics versus Progrrammatic Politics.' Working Paper. Harvard University.

Barkley, K. (2008) *The Ottomans in Comparative Perspective*. Cambridge, UK: Cambridge University Press.

Basu, K. (2000) *Prelude to Political Economy*. Oxford: Oxford University Press. https://doi.org/10.1093/0198296711.001.0001.

(2005) 'Racial Conflict and the Malignancy of Identity.' *Journal of Economic Inequality* 3: 221–241. https://doi.org/10.1007/s10888-005-9002-8.

(2011) *Beyond the Invisible Hand: Groundwork for a New Economics*. Princeton, NJ: Princeton University Press.

(2021) 'Hume and Hobbes, with a Dash of Nash: Why have Leaders at All?' Working Paper, Department of Economics, Cornell University.

Battilana, J., B. Leca and E. Boxenbaum (2014) 'How Actors Change Institutions: Towards a Theory of Institutional Entrepreneurship.' *The Academy of Management Annals* 3(1): 65–107. https://doi.org/10.1080/19416520903053598.

Bebbington, A., A. G. Abdulai, D. Humphreys Bebbington, M. Hinfelaar, and C. A. Sanborn (2018) *Governing Extractive Industries: Politics, History, Ideas*. Oxford: Oxford University Press. https://doi.org/10.1093/oso/9780198820932.001.0001.

Behuria, P. (2025) 'Donors and Disciplines Meet the Political Economy of Development: The Contested Evolution of Political Settlements Analysis.' *Progress in Development Studies* 1–22. https://doi.org/10.1177/14649934251322274.

Benabou, R. (2008) *Ideology*. National Bureau of Economic Research Working Paper 13907. www.nber.org/papers/w13907.

Ben-Ghiat, R. (2020) *Strongmen: Mussolini to the Present*. New York: W. W. Norton.

Bernhard, H., E. Fehr and U. Fischbacher (2006) 'Group Affiliation and Altruistic Norm Enforcement.' *American Economic Reivew* 96(2): 217–221. https://doi.org/10.1257/000282806777212594.

Block, R. (1993) 'Killers.' *The New York Review of Books* 40(19): 9–10.
Blumer, H. (1958) 'Race Prejudice as a Sense of Group Position.' *Pacific Sociological Review* 1(1): 3–7. https://doi.org/10.2307/1388607.
Boissevain, J. (1965) *Saints and Fireworks: Religion and Politics in Rural Malta*. London: Athlone.
Boschini, A. D., J. Pettersson, and J. Roine (2007) 'Resource Curse or Not: A Question of Appropriability.' *The Scandinavian Journal of Economics* 109(3): 593–617. https://doi.org/10.1111/j.1467-9442.2007.00509.x.
Bowles, S. (1985) 'The Production Process in a Competitive Economy: Walrasian, Neo-Hobbesian, and Marxian Models.' *American Economic Reivew* 75(5): 16–36.
   (1998) 'Endogenous Preferences: The Cultural Consequences of Markets and other Economic Institutions.' *Journal of Economic Literature* 36: 75–111.
   (2004) *Microeconomics: Behavior, Institutions, and Evolution*. Princeton, NJ: Princeton University Press.
Bowles S. and H. Gintis (1992) 'Power and Wealth in a Competitive Capitalist Economy.' *Philosophy and Public Affairs* 21(4): 324–353.
Bowles S. and H. Gintis (2008) 'Power.' In S. Durlauf and L. E. Blume (Eds.) *The New Palgrave Dictionary of Economics*, 2nd Ed. New York: Palgrave Macmillan, Vol. 6: 565–570.
Bradbury, M. (2008) *Becoming Somaliland*. Bloomington, IN: Indiana University Press.
Brewer, M. B. and W. Gardner (1996) 'Who Is this "We"? Levels of collective identity and self representations.' *Journal of Personality and Social Psychology*, 71(1), 83–93. https://doi.org/10.1037/0022-3514.71.1.83.
Bruneau, E. G., M. Cikara, and R. Saxe (2017) 'Parochial Empathy Predicts Reduced Altruism and the Endorsement of Passive Harm.' *Social Psychological and Personality Science* 8(8): 934–942. https://doi.org/10.1177/1948550617693064.
Burke, M. and P. Young (2009) 'Social Norms.' in A. Bisin, J. Benhibib, and M. Jackson (Eds.) *The Handbook of Social Economics*. Amsterdam: North-Holland: 311–338.
Carbone, G. (2009) 'The Consequences of Democratization.' *Journal of Democracy* 20(2): 123–137. https://doi.org/10.1353/jod.0.0085.
Chamberlain, N. W. and J. W. Kuhn (1965) *Collective Bargaining*. New York: McGraw Hill.
Cleaver, F. (2002) 'Reinventing Institutions: Bricolage and the Social Embeddedness of Natural Resource Management.' *European Journal of Development Research* 14(2): 11–30. https://doi.org/10.1080/714000425.

Corbett, J. (2019) 'Where do Leaders Come From? A Leader-Centered Approach.' Development Leadership Program (DLP) Foundational Paper.

Crawford, S. and E. Ostrom (2005) 'A Grammar of Institutions.' In E. Ostrom (Ed.) *Understanding Institutional Diversity*, Princeton, NJ: Princeton University Press: 137–174.

Crenshaw, K. (1989) 'Demarginalizing the Intersection of Race and Sex: A Black Feminist Critique of Antidiscrimination Doctrine, Feminist Theory and Antiracist Politics.' *University of Chicago Legal Forum* 129: 139–167

Crouch. C. (2005) *Capitalist Diversity and Change: Recombinant Governance and Institutional Entrepreneurs*. Oxford: Oxford University Press. https://doi.org/10.1093/acprof:oso/9780199286652.002.0003.

Cyert, J. G. and R. M. March (1963) *A Behavioral Theory of the Firm*. Englewood Cliffs, NJ: Prentice Hall.

Dahl, R. (1957) 'The Concept of Power.' *Behavioral Science* 2: 201–215. https://doi.org/10.1002/bs.3830020303.

(1961) *Who Governs: Democracy and Power in an American City*. New Haven, CT: Yale University Press.

Darity, W. A. and J. B. Stewart (2006) 'Economics of Identity Origin and Persistence of Racial Identity Norms.' *Journal of Economic Behavior and Organization* 60: 283–305. https://doi.org/10.1016/j.jebo.2004.09.005.

Darity, W. A. Jr., D. Hamilton, P. L. Mason, et al. (2017) 'Stratification Economics: A General Theory of Intergroup Inequality.' In Chapter 2 of Flynn, Andrea, S. R. Holmbert, D. T. Warren and F. J. Wong (Eds.) *The Hidden Rules of Race: Barriers to an Inclusive Economy*. Cambridge: Cambridge University Press: 35–51. https://doi.org/10.1017/9781108277846.003.

Darity, W. A. Jr., P. L. Mason, and J. B. Stewart (2013) 'The Economics of Identity: The Origin and Persistence of Racial Identity Norms.' *Journal of Economic Behavior and Organization* 60: 283–305. https://doi.org/10.1016/j.jebo.2004.09.005.

Davis, J. B. (2015) 'Stratification Economics and Identity Economics.' *Cambridge Journal of Economics* 39(5): 1215–1229. https://doi.org/10.1093/cje/beu071.

Dawkins, R. (1976) *The Selfish Gene*. Oxford: Oxford University Press.

de Mesquita, E. B. (2010) 'Regime Change and Revolutionary Entrepreneurs.' *American Political Science Review* 104(3): 446–467. https://doi.org/10.1017/S0003055410000274.

Denzau, A, T. and D. C. North (1994) 'Shared Mental Models: Ideologies and Institutions.' *Kyklos* 47(1): 3–31.

Dew, N., D. D. Sarasvathy, and S. Venkataraman (2004) 'The Economic Implications of Exaptation.' *Journal of Evolutionary Economics* 14: 69–84. https://doi.org/10.1007/s00191-003-0180-x.

Di John, J. and J. Putzel (2009) *Political Settlements: Issues Paper*. Discussion Paper. Birmingham: University of Birmingham.

DiMaggio, P. J. and W. W. Powell (1983) 'The Iron Cage Revisited: Institutional Isomorphism and Collective Rationality in Organizational Fields.' *American Sociological Review* 48(2): 147–160. https://doi.org/10.2307/2095101.

DiMaggio, P. (1988) 'Interest and Agency in Institutional Theory.' In Lynne G. Zucker, (Ed.) *Research on Institutional Patterns: Environment and Culture*. Cambridge: Ballinger.

Dixit, A. (2021) 'Somewhere in the Middle You Can Survive.' *Journal of Economic Literature* 59(4): 1361–1375.

Doner, R. F., B. K. Ritchie, and D. Slater (2005) 'Systemic Vulnerability and the Origins of Developmental States: Northeast and Southeast Asia in Comparative Perspective.' *International Organization* 59: 327–361.

Doner, R. F. and B. R. Schneider (2016) 'The Middle-Income Trap: More Politics than Economics.' *World Politics* 4: 608–644. https://doi.org/10.1017/S0043887116000095.

Downs, A. (1957) 'Up and Down with Ecology: The Issue Attention Cycle.' *Public Interest* 28: 38–50.

Eisenstadt and Roniger (1980) 'Patient-Client Relations as a Model of Structuring Social Exchange.' *Comparative Studies in Society and History* 22(1): 42–77. https://doi.org/10.1017/S0010417500009154.

Elster, J. (1989) *The Cement of Society: A Study of Social Order*. Cambridge: Cambridge University Press.

Engerman, S. L. and K. L. and Sokolof (2002) 'Factor Endowments, Inequality, and Paths of Development among New World Economies. *Economia* 3(*1*): 41–109. https://doi.org/10.1353/eco.2002.0013.

Escobal, J., V. Agreda, and T. Reardon (2000) 'Endogenous Institutional Innovation and Agroindustrialization on the Peruvian Coast.' *Agricultural Economics* 23: 267–277. https://doi.org/10.22004/ag.econ.176213.

Evans, P. (2011) 'Constructing the 21st Century Developmental State'. Mimeo.

Fearon, J. D. and D. D. Laitin (2000) 'Violence and the Social Construction of Ethnic Identity.' *International Organization* 54(04): 845–877. https://doi.org/10.1162/002081800551398.

Ferguson, W. D. (2013) *Collective Action and Exchange: A Game-Theoretic Approach to Political Economy*. Stanford, CA: Stanford University Press. https://doi.org/10.1515/9780804785563.

Ferguson, W. D. (2019) 'Facing Uncertainty: Norms and Formal Institutions as Shared Mental Models.' SSRN Working Paper. http://dx.doi.org/10.2139/ssrn.3410109.

(2020) *The Political Economy of Collective Action, Inequality, and Development*. Stanford, CA: Stanford University Press. https://doi.org/10.1515/9781503611979.

(2024) 'Power and Public Authority.' *Global Policy 15(S4)* Special Issue: Development Practice, Power, and Public Authority: 11–23. https://doi.org/10.1111/1758-5899.13205.

Folbre, N. (2014) 'The Care Economy in Africa: Subsistence Production and Unpaid Care.' *Journal of African Economies* 23: 128–156. https://doi.org/10.1093/jae/ejt026.

(2006) 'Measuring Care: Gender, Empowerment, and the Care Economy.' *Journal of Human Development* 7(2): 183–200. https://doi.org/10.1080/14649880600768512.

Gartzou-Katsouyanni, K. (2024) 'How Can Public Policies Facilitate Local Cooperation? Insights from the EU's Wine Policy.' *New Political Economy* 597–695, https://doi.org/10.1080/13563467.2024.2305252.

Gaventa, J. (1980) *Power and Powerlessness: Quiescence and Rebellion in an Appalachian Valley*. Urbana, IA: University of Illinois Press.

Gil, I. S. and H. Kharas (2015) 'The Middle-Income Trap Turns Ten.' Policy Research Working Paper 7403. World Bank Group.

Gintis, H. (2009) *The Bounds of Reason*. Princeton, NJ: Princeton University Press.

Gĩthĩnji, M. (2015) 'Erasing Class/(RE)Creating Ethnicity: Jobs, Politics, Accumulation, and Identity in Kenya.' *Review of Black Political Economy* 42: 87–110. https://doi.org/10.1007/s12114-014-9191-0.

Glaeser, E. L. (2005) 'The Political Economy of Hatred.' *The Quarterly Journal of Economics* 120(1): 45–86. https://doi.org/10.1162/0033553053327434.

Goodhand and Walton (2022) 'Fixes and Flux: Frontier Brokers, Political Settlements and Post-War Politics in Nepal and Sri Lanka.' *The Journal of Development Studies* 58(11): 2331–2348, https://doi.org/10.1080/00220388.2022.2086046.

Gould S. J. (2002) *The Structure of Evolutionary Theory*. Cambridge, MA: Belknap. https://doi.org/10.4159/9780674417922.

Gould, S. J. and E. S. Vrba (1982) 'Exaptation – A Missing Term in the Science of Form.' *Paleobiology* 8(1): 4–15. https://doi.org/10.1017/S0094837300004310.

Greif, A. (2006) *Institutions and the Path to the Modern Economy: Lessons from Medieval Trade*. Cambridge: Cambridge University Press. https://doi.org/10.1017/CBO9780511791307

Grillitich, M. and M. Sotaratua (2020) 'Trinity of Change Agency, Regional Development Paths and Opportunity Spaces.' *Progress in Human Geography* 44(4)S: 704–723. https://doi.org/10.1177/0309132519853870.

Haber, S., A. Razo, and N. Maurer (2003) *The Politics of Property Rights: Political Instability, Credible Commitments, and Economic Growth in Mexico (1876–1929)*, Cambridge: Cambridge University Press.

Hale, H. A. (2008) *Foundations of Ethnic Politics: Separatism of States and Nations in Eurasia and the World*. Cambridge: Cambridge University Press. https://doi.org/10.1017/CBO9780511790669.

Hall, P. A. and K. Thelen (2009) 'Institutional Change in Varieties of Capitalism.' *Socio-Economic Review* 7: 7–34. https://doi.org/10.1093/ser/mwn020.

Harris, J. R. and M. P. Todaro (1970) 'Migration, Unemployment, and Development: A Two-Sector Model.' *American Economic Review* 60(1): 126–142.

Harsanyi, J. (1977) *Rational Behaviour and Bargaining Equilibrium in Games and Social Situations*. Cambridge: Cambridge University Press.

Hendrickson, M. and T. Sanandaji (2010) T*he Interaction of Entrepreneurship and Institutions*. IFN Working Paper No. 830.

Hickey, S. and K. Sen (2024) *Pathways to Development: From Politics to Power*. Oxford: Oxford University Press. https://doi.org/10.1093/oso/9780198872566.001.0001.

Hickey, S., K. Sen, and B. Bukenya (eds.) (2014) *The Politics of Inclusive Development: Interrogating the Evidence*. Oxford: Oxford University Press. https://doi.org/10.1093/acprof:oso/9780198722564.001.0001.

Hobbes, T. (1668) *Leviathan*. 2017 ed., Christopher Booke. London: Penguin.

Hogg, M., D. Terry, and K. White (1995) 'A Tale of Two Theories: A Critical Comparison of Identity Theory with Social Identity Theory.' *Social Psychology Quarterly* 58: 255–269. https://doi.org/10.2307/2787127.

Horowitz, D. (1985) *Ethnic Groups in Conflict*. Berkeley, CA: University of California Press.

Hudson, D. and C. McLoughlin (2019) 'How is Leadership Understood in Different Contexts? Development Leadership Program (DLP) Foundational Paper 1.

Hume, D. (1758) 'Of the First Principles of Government.' In *Essays: Moral, Political and Literary*. [1987 edition by Liberty Fund, Indianapolis.]

Hussein, J. (2025) The Dynamics of Collective Action and Political Settlements: A Comparative Study of Somaliland and Somalia. DIA Thesis, Johns Hopkins University, Baltimore, MD.

Hutchinson and Pendle (2015) 'Violence, Legitimacy, and Prophecy: Nuer Struggles with Uncertainty in South Sudan.' *American Ethnologist* 42(3): 415–430. https://doi.org/10.1111/amet.12138.

James D. (2011) 'The Return of the Broker: Consensus, Hierarchy and Choice in SA Land Reform.' *Journal of the Royal Anthropological Institute* (N.S.) 17: 318–338. https://doi.org/10.1111/j.1467-9655.2011.01682.x

Kahneman, D. (2003) 'Maps of Bounded Rationality: Psychology for Behavioral Economics.' *American Economic Review* 93(5): 1449–1475. https://doi.org/10.1257/000282803322655392.

Kelsall, T., and M. vom Hau (2019) 'Beyond Institutions: A Political Settlements Approach to Development.' Institut Barcelona d'Estudis Internationals: IBEI Working Papers, 56.

Kelsall, T., N. Schulz, W. D. Ferguson, M. vom Hau, S. Hickey, and B. Levy (2022) *Political Settlements and Development: Theory, Evidence, Implications*. Oxford: Oxford University Press. https://doi.org/10.1093/oso/9780192848932.001.0001.

Khan, M. (2010) 'Political Settlements and the Governance of Growth-Enhancing Institutions'. *Draft Paper in Research Paper Series on 'Growth-Enhancing Governance'*. (Unpublished)

Khan, M. (2018) 'Political Settlements and the Analysis of Institutions.' *African Affairs* 117(469): 636–655.

Kirk, T. (2024) 'Intermediaries, Isomorphic Activism and Programming for Social Accountability in Pakistan.' *Global Policy 15(S4) Special Issue: Development Practice, Power, and Public Authority*: 60–70. https://doi.org/10.1111/1758-5899.13218.

Kirk, T. and R. Pennington (2024) 'Introduction: Development Practice, Power and Public Authority.' *Global Policy 15(S4) Special Issue: Development Practice, Power, and Public Authority*: 5–10. https://doi.org/10.1111/1758-5899.13393.

Knight, J. (1992) Institutions and Social Conflict. Cambridge: Cambridge University Press.

Kosters and Leynseele (2018) 'Brokers as Assemblers: Studying Development Through the Lens of Brokerage.' *Ethnos* 83(5): 803–813. https://doi.org/10.1080/00141844.2017.1362451.

Kuran, T. (1995) *Private Truths Public Lies: The Social Consequences of Preference Falsification*. Cambridge, MA: Harvard University Press.

Laswell (1936) *Politics: Who Gets What, When, and How?* New York: McGraw Hill.

Laws E. L. (2012) 'Political Settlements, Elite Pacts, and Government of National Unity: A Conceptual Study.' DLP Background Paper 10. Development Leadership Program, University of Birmingham. www.dlprog.org.

Laws, E. and A. Leftwich (2014) 'Political Settlements.' DLP Concept Brief. Development Leadership Program, University of Birmingham. www.dlprog.org.

Leftwich, A. (2010) 'Beyond Institutions: Rethinking the Role of Leaders, Elites and Coalitions in the Institutional Formation of Developmental States and Strategies.' *Forum for Development Studies*, 37(1): 93–111, https://doi.org/10.1080/08039410903558327.

Lenin, V. I. (1939) *Imperialism, the Highest Stage of Capitalism: A Popular Outline*. New York: International Publishers.

Levi, M. (2025) 'Expanding the Community of Fate by Expanding the Community of Care.' *Daedalus*, Winter: 240–250. https://doi.org/10.1162/daed_a_02135.

Levi-Strauss, C. (1966) *The Savage Mind*. English Translation George Widenfeld, and Nicholson Ltd. Chicago, IL: University of Chicago Press.

Levy, B. (2013) 'Seeking the Elusive Developmental Knife Edge: Zambia and Mozambique – A Tale of Two Countries.' In D. C. North, J. H. Wallis, S. G. Webb and B. R. Weingast (Eds.) *The Shadow of Violence: Politics, Economics, and the Problems of Development*. Cambridge: Cambridge University Press: 112–148. https://doi.org/10.1017/CBO9781139013611.004.

Levy, B. (2014) *Working with the Grain: Integrating Governance and Growth in Development Strategies*. Oxford: Oxford University Press. https://doi.org/10.1093/acprof:oso/9780199363803.001.0001.

Levy, B. and F. Fukuyama (2010) *Development Strategies: Integrating Governance and Growth*. World Bank Policy Research Working Paper 5196.

Levy, B., A. Hirsch, V. Naidoo, and M. Nxele (2021) *South Africa: When Strong Institutions and Massive Inequalities Collide*. Paper. Carnegie Endowment for International Peace.

Lin, J. Y. (2012) *New Structural Economics: A Framework for Rethinking Development and Policy*. Washington, DC: World Bank. https://doi.org/10.1596/978-0-8213-8955-3.

Lindquist, J., B. Xiang, and B. S. A. Yeoh (2012) 'Introduction: Opening the Black Box of Migration: Brokers, the Organization of Transnational Mobility and the Changing Political Economy in Asia.' *Pacific Affairs* 85(1): 7–19. https://doi.org/132.161.214.20.

Lukes, S. (1974) *Power: A Radical View*. London: Macmillan.

Lust, E. M. (2022) *Everyday Choices: The Role of Competing Authorities and Social Institutions in Politics and Development*. Cambridge Elements in Politics of Development. Cambridge: Cambridge University Press. https://doi.org/10.1017/9781009306164.

Mahoney and Thelen (2009) 'A Theory of Gradual Institutional Change.' In Mahoney and Thelen (Eds.) *Explaining Institutional Change: Ambiguity, Agency, and Power*. Cambridge: Cambridge University Press, 1–38. https://doi.org/10.1017/CBO9780511806414.003.

Mandela, N. (1953) *No Easy Walk to Freedom. Presidential address to the ANC [African National Congress (Transvaal) Conference, September 21, 1953*.

Mandela, N. (1965) *No Easy Walk to Freedom*. Oxford: Heinemann, International.

Mandela, N. (1986) *The Struggle Is My Life*. London: International Defense and Aid Fund.

Mandela, N. (1994) *Long Walk to Freedom: The Autobiography of Nelson Mandela*. Boston, MA: Little Brown and Company.

Matland. R. E. (1995) 'Synthesizing the Implementation Literature: The Ambiguity-Conflict Model of Policy Implementation.' *Journal of Public Administration Research and Theory* 5(2): 145–174. https://doi.org/10.1093/oxfordjournals.jpart.a037242.

Meehan, P. and S. Plonski (2017) 'Brokering the Martins: A Review of Conceptions and Methods.' Working Paper 1, SOAS and the University of Bath.

Menkhaus, K. (2018) 'Neither War nor Peace in Somalia'. *Journal of East African* 12(1): 1–19.

Miller J. H. and S. E. Page (2007) *Complex Adaptive Systems*. Princeton, NJ: Princeton University Press. https://doi.org/10.1515/9781400835522.

Mody, A. (2023) *India Is Broken*. Stanford, CA: Stanford University Press.

Mokyr, J. (2000) 'Evolutionary Phenomena in Technological Change.' In J. Ziman (Ed.) *Technological Innovation as an Evolutionary Process*. Cambridge: Cambridge University Press, 52–65.

Mukand, S. and D. Rodrick (2018) *The Political Economy of Ideas: On Ideas Versus Interests in Policymaking*. NBER Working Paper 24467.

North, D. (1990) *Institutions, Institutional Change, and Economic Performance*. Cambridge: Cambridge University Press. https://doi.org/10.1017/CBO9780511808678.

Oleinik, A. (2016) *The Invisible Hand of Power: An Economic Theory of Gatekeeping*. New York: Routledge.

Olson, M. (1965) *The Logic of Collective Action: Public Goods and The Theory of Groups*. Cambridge, MA: Harvard University Press.

Ostrom, E. (1990) *Governing the Commons: The Evolution of Institutions for Collective Action*. Cambridge: Cambridge University Press.

Ostrom, V. and E. Ostrom (1977) 'Public Goods and Public Choices.' In E. S. Savas (Ed.) *Delivering Public Services: Toward Improved Performances*. Boulder, CO: Westview, 7–49. https://doi.org/10.4324/9780429047978-2.

Pacheo, D., J. G. York, T. J. Dean, and S. D. Sarasvathy (2010) 'The Coevolution of Institutional Entrepreneurship: A Tale of Two Theories.' *Journal of Management* 36(4): 974–1010. https://doi.org/10.1177/0149206309360280.

Phillips, S. (2013) 'Political Settlements and State Formation: The Case of Somaliland.' Developmental Leadership Program.

Piketty, T. (2020) *Capital and Ideology*. Cambridge, MA: Harvard University Press.

Raeymakers, T. K. (2010) 'Protection for Sale? War and Transformation of Regulation on the Congo-Ugandan Border.' *Development and Change* 41(4): 563–587. https://doi.org/10.1111/j.1467-7660.2010.01655.x.

Randeraad, N. (1998) 'Introduction.' In N. Randeraad (Ed.) *Mediators between State and Society*. Hilversum: Verloren, 8–16.

Ransom, R. L. and R. Sutch (2001) *One Kind of Freedom: The Economic Consequences of Emancipation*. 2nd ed. Cambridge: Cambridge University Press. https://doi.org/10.1017/CBO9780511812385.

Riker, W. (1962) *The Theory of Political Coalitions*. New Haven, CT: Yale University Press.

Rodrik, D. (2013) *Structural Change Fundamentals and Growth: An Overview*. Princeton, NJ: Institute for Advanced Study.

Rodrik, D. (2014) 'The Past, Present, and Future of Economic Growth.' In F. Allen, J. R. Behrman, N. Birdsall, et al. (Eds.), *Towards a Better Global Economy: Policy Implications for Citizens Worldwide in the 21st Century*. Oxford: Oxford University Press: 70–137. https://doi.org/10.1093/acprof:oso/9780198723455.001.0001.

Rodrik, D. (2016) 'Premature Deindustrialization.' *Journal of Economic Growth* 21(1), 1–33. https://doi.org/10.1007/s10887-015-9122-3.

Sabatier, P. A. and H. Jenkins-Smith (1998) 'An Advocacy Coalition Model of Policy Change and the Role of Policy Oriented Learning Therein.' *Western Political Quarterly* 41: 449–476.

Sambanis, N. and M. Shayo (2013) 'Social Identification and Ethnic Conflict.' *American Political Science Review* 107(2): 294–325. https://doi.org/10.1017/S0003055413000038.

Sarasvathy, S. D. (2001) 'Causation and Effectuation: Toward a Theoretical Shift from Economic Inevitability to Entrepreneurial Contingency.' *Academy of Management Review* 26(2): 243–263. https://doi.org/10.2307/259121.

Sarasvathy, S.D. (2008). *Effectuation: Elements of Entrepreneurial Expertise*. Northampton, MA: Edward Elgar.

Schatschneider, E. E. (1960) *The Semisovereign People: A Realist's View of Democracy in America*. 1st ed. New York: Holt, Reinhart, and Winston.

Schelling, T. (1960) *Strategy of Conflict*. Cambridge, MA: Harvard University Press.

Scott, J. C. (1998) *Seeing Like a State: How Certain Schemes to Improve the Human Condition Have Failed*. New Haven, CT: Yale University Press. https://doi.org/10.12987/9780300128789.

Sen, A. (1999) *Development as Freedom*. New York: Random House.

Sen, A. (2006) *Identity and Violence: The Illusion of Destiny*. New York: Norton.

Sen, K. (2019) 'Structural Transformation around the World: Patterns and Drivers.' *Asian Development Review* 36(2): 1–31. https://doi.org/10.1162/adev_a_00130.

(2023) *Varieties of Structural Transformation*. Cambridge: Cambridge University Press. https://doi.org/10.1017/9781009449939.

Shayo, M. (2009) 'A Model of Social Identity with an Application to Political Economy: Nation, Class, and Redistribution.' *American Political Science Review* 103(2): 147–174. https://doi.org/10.1017/S0003055409090194.

Shepsle, K. A. and R. Noll (1985) 'Comment of Why the Regulators Chose to Deregulate.' in R. G. Noll (Ed.) *Regulatory Policy and the Social Sciences*. Berkley, CA: University of California Press: 231–239.

Simmel, G. (1902) 'The Number of Members as Determining the Sociological Form of the Group: II.' *American Journal of Sociology* 8(1): 58–196.

Slater, D. (2010) *Ordering Power: Contentious Politics and Authoritarian Leviathans in Southeast Asia*. Cambridge: Cambridge University Press. https://doi.org/10.1017/CBO9780511760891.

Solnick, S. and D. Hemenway (1998) 'Is More Always Better: A Survey on Positional Concerns.' *Journal of Economic Behavior and Organization* 37(3): 373–383. https://doi.org/10.1016/S0167-2681(98)00089-4.

Spence, M. (2011) *The Next Convergence. The Future of Economic Growth in a Multispeed World*. New York: Farrar, Straus and Giroux.

Stiglitz, J. (1987) 'The Causes and Consequences of the Dependence of Quality on Price.' *Journal of Economic Literature* 25: 1–48.

Stiglitz, J. and A. Weiss (1981) 'Credit Rationing in Markets with Imperfect Information.' *American Economic Review* 71(3): 393–410.

Stovel, K. and L. Shaw (2012) 'Brokerage.' *Annual Review of Sociology* 38: 139–158. https://doi.org/10.1146/annurev-soc-081309-150054.

Sunstein, C. (1996) 'Social Norms and Socia Roles.' *Columbia Law Review* 96: 903–968. https://doi.org/10.2307/1123430.

Tapscott, R. (2017) 'The Government Has Long Hands: Institutionalized Arbitrariness and Local Security Initiatives in Northern Uganda.' *Development and Change* 48(2): 263–285. https://doi.org/10.1111/dech.12294.

Taylor, M. (1982) *Community, Anarchy, and Liberty*. Cambridge: Cambridge University Press.

Thoits, P. and L. Virshup (1997) 'Me's and We's: Forms and Functions of Social Identities.' In R. Ashmore and L. Jussim (Eds.) *Self and Identity: Fundamental Issues*, 1, Oxford: Oxford University Press, 106–133. https://doi.org/10.1093/oso/9780195098266.003.0005.

Tilly, C. and S. Tarrow (2015) *Contentious Politics*. 2nd ed. Oxford: Oxford University Press.

Tudor, M. and A. Ziegfeld (2019) 'Social Cleavages, Party Organization, and the End of Single-Party Dominance: Insights from India.' *Comparative Politics* 52(1): 149–168.

Veblen, T. [1899] (2005). *The Theory of the Leisure Class: An Economic Study of Institutions*. Deli: Aakar Books.

Walter, B. F. (2023) *How Civil Wars Start and How to Stop Them*. New York: Crown Trade.

Williamson, O. (1979) 'Transaction-Cost Economics: The Governance of Contractual Relations.' *Journal of Law and Economics* 22(2): 233–261. https://doi.org/10.1086/466942.

Wolf, E. R. (1956) 'Aspects of Group Relations in a Complex Society: Mexico.' *American Anthropologist* 58(6): 1065–1078. https://doi.org/10.1525/aa.1956.58.6.02a00070.

Wright, E. O. (1978) *Class, Crisis, and the State*. London: New Left Books.

Acknowledgements

I thank Elements in Development Economics series editor, Kunal Sen, for his encouragement, delightful conversations, comments, for sponsoring my visit to UNU-WIDER, and for coordinating this publication. I thank Eric Beinhocker and Kaushik Basu for sponsoring my several academic visits, respectively, at the Oxford Institute for New Economic Thinking and the Cornell University Department of Economics. I thank them both for many useful conversations and seminars related to developmental dilemmas, agency, and power. I offer similar thanks to Gerald Epstein and Robert Pollin for arranging my visit to the Political Economy Research Institute at the University of Massachusetts, Amherst. At all four institutions, my time as a visiting scholar offered useful conversations with scholars, feedback on my talks, and useful seminars from many researchers, all of which facilitated my work on this project. I thank Michael Woolcock and Timothy Williamson for arranging my talk at the World Bank, from which I received useful feedback.

As I worked out key concepts related to this Element, I benefited from comments, conversations, and/or correspondence with multiple scholars including, Janie Aaron, Richard Bailey, Charles Becker, Tim Besley, Sam Bowles, James Boyce, Wendy Carlin, Daniel Chandler, Stefan Dercon, Nancy Folbre, Kira Gartzou-Katsouyanni, Rachel Gisselquist, Jayati Ghosh, Peter Hall, Sam Hickey, Tim Kelsall, Don Katzner, Tom Kirk, Margaret Levi, Brian Levy, Patrick Mason, Léonce Ndikumana, Dani Rodrik, Pallavi Roy, Isabel Ruiz, Nicollai Schultz, Dennis Snower, Maya Tudor, Matthias vom Hau, and Ben Zissimos. Many conversations with the late Elinor Ostrom informed my understanding of collective-action problems. The late Herbert Gintis shaped my approach to game-theoretic reasoning. I also thank two anonymous referees for extremely useful comments.

I thank Grinnell College, and especially the Committee in Support of Faculty Scholarship, for their generous support for multiple scholarly visits. I thank President Anne Harris for her enthusiastic encouragement. I thank Susan Ferrari for her encouragement and for sponsoring workshops related to presenting one's scholarship. I thank the Grinnell Economics Department chairs, Eric Ohrn and Logan Lee, for their support. I thank my faculty colleagues Barry Driscoll, Tammy McGavock, and Mark Montgomery for their encouragement. I appreciate the technical assistance provided by Grinnell's Cheryl Fleener-Seymore, Angie Vander Leest, Morris Pelzel, and Laurie Wilcox. I thank UNU-Wider and CUP staff, including Adam Hopper, Siméon Rapin, and Sowmya

Singaravelu, for their assistance with preparations. I give a special thanks to Sam Cox for providing a wonderful writing environment at Saint's Rest Coffee House in Grinnell, Iowa. Last, and certainly not least, I offer loving thanks to my wife, Claudia Beckwith, for her love, encouragement, and support as I worked on this project.

Cambridge Elements

Development Economics

Series Editor-in-Chief
Kunal Sen
UNU-WIDER and University of Manchester

Kunal Sen, UNU-WIDER Director, is Editor-in-Chief of the Cambridge Elements in Development Economics series. Professor Sen has over three decades of experience in academic and applied development economics research, and has carried out extensive work on international finance, the political economy of inclusive growth, the dynamics of poverty, social exclusion, female labour force participation, and the informal sector in developing economies. His research has focused on India, East Asia, and sub-Saharan Africa.

In addition to his work as Professor of Development Economics at the University of Manchester, Kunal has been the Joint Research Director of the Effective States and Inclusive Development (ESID) Research Centre, and a Research Fellow at the Institute for Labor Economics (IZA). He has also served in advisory roles with national governments and bilateral and multilateral development agencies, including the UK's Department for International Development, Asian Development Bank, and the International Development Research Centre.

Thematic Editors
Tony Addison
University of Copenhagen and UNU-WIDER

Tony Addison is a Professor of Economics in the University of Copenhagen's Development Economics Research Group. He is also a Non-Resident Senior Research Fellow at UNU-WIDER, Helsinki, where he was previously the Chief Economist-Deputy Director. In addition, he is Professor of Development Studies at the University of Manchester. His research interests focus on the extractive industries, energy transition, and macroeconomic policy for development.

Chris Barrett
SC Johnson College of Business, Cornell University

Chris Barrett is an agricultural and development economist at Cornell University. He is the Stephen B. and Janice G. Ashley Professor of Applied Economics and Management and International Professor of Agriculture at the Charles H. Dyson School of Applied Economics and Management. He is also an elected Fellow of the American Association for the Advancement of Science, the Agricultural and Applied Economics Association, and the African Association of Agricultural Economists.

Carlos Gradín
University of Vigo

Carlos Gradín is a professor of applied economics at the University of Vigo. His main research interest is the study of inequalities, with special attention to those that exist between population groups (e.g., by race or sex). His publications have contributed to improving the empirical evidence in developing and developed countries, as well as globally, and to improving the available data and methods used.

Rachel M. Gisselquist
UNU-WIDER

Rachel M. Gisselquist is a Senior Research Fellow and member of the Senior Management Team of UNU-WIDER. She specializes in the comparative politics of developing countries, with particular attention to issues of inequality, ethnic and identity politics, foreign aid and state building, democracy and governance, and sub-Saharan African politics. Dr Gisselquist has edited a dozen collections in these areas, and her articles are published in a range of leading journals.

Shareen Joshi
Georgetown University

Shareen Joshi is an Associate Professor of International Development at Georgetown University's School of Foreign Service in the United States. Her research focuses on issues of inequality, human capital investment, and grassroots collective action in South Asia. Her work has been published in the fields of development economics, population studies, environmental studies, and gender studies.

Patricia Justino
UNU-WIDER and IDS – UK

Patricia Justino is a Senior Research Fellow at UNU-WIDER and Professorial Fellow at the Institute of Development Studies (IDS) (on leave). Her research focuses on the relationship between political violence, governance, and development outcomes. She has published widely in the fields of development economics and political economy and is the co-founder and co-director of the Households in Conflict Network (HiCN).

Marinella Leone
University of Pavia

Marinella Leone is an assistant professor at the Department of Economics and Management, University of Pavia, Italy. She is an applied development economist. Her more recent research focuses on the study of early child development parenting programmes, on education, and gender-based violence. In previous research, she investigated the short, long-term and intergenerational impact of conflicts on health, education and domestic violence. She has published in top journals in economics and development economics.

Jukka Pirttilä
University of Helsinki and UNU-WIDER

Jukka Pirttilä is Professor of Public Economics at the University of Helsinki and VATT Institute for Economic Research. He is also a Non-Resident Senior Research Fellow at UNU-WIDER. His research focuses on tax policy, especially for developing countries. He is a co-principal investigator at the Finnish Centre of Excellence in Tax Systems Research.

Andy Sumner
King's College London and UNU-WIDER

Andy Sumner is Professor of International Development at King's College London; a Non-Resident Senior Fellow at UNU-WIDER and a Fellow of the Academy of Social Sciences. He has published extensively in the areas of poverty, inequality, and economic development.

About the Series

Cambridge Elements in Development Economics is led by UNU-WIDER in partnership with Cambridge University Press. The series publishes authoritative studies on important topics in the field covering both micro and macro aspects of development economics.

United Nations University World Institute for Development Economics Research

United Nations University World Institute for Development Economics Research (UNU-WIDER) provides economic analysis and policy advice aiming to promote sustainable and equitable development for all. The institute began operations in 1985 in Helsinki, Finland, as the first research centre of the United Nations University. Today, it is one of the world's leading development economics think tanks, working closely with a vast network of academic researchers and policy makers, mostly based in the Global South.

Cambridge Elements

Development Economics

Elements in the Series

Varieties of Structural Transformation: Patterns, Determinants, and Consequences
Kunal Sen

Economic Transformation and Income Distribution in China over Three Decades
Cai Meng, Bjorn Gustafsson and John Knight

Chilean Economic Development under Neoliberalism: Structural Transformation, High Inequality and Environmental Fragility
Andrés Solimano and Gabriela Zapata-Román

Hierarchy of Needs and the Measurement of Poverty and Standards of Living
Joseph Deutsch and Jacques Silber

New Structural Financial Economics: A Framework for Rethinking the Role of Finance in Serving the Real Economy
Justin Yifu Lin, Jiajun Xu, Zirong Yang and Yilin Zhang

Knowledge and Global Inequality Since 1800: Interrogating the Present as History
Dev Nathan

Survival of the Greenest: Economic Transformation in a Climate-conscious World
Amir Lebdioui

Escaping Poverty Traps and Unlocking Prosperity in the Face of Climate Risk: Lessons from Index-Based Livestock Insurance
Nathaniel D. Jensen, Francesco P. Fava, Andrew G. Mude, Christopher B. Barrett, Brenda Wandera-Gache, Anton Vrieling, Masresha Taye, Kazushi Takahashi, Felix Lung, Munenobu Ikegami, Polly Ericksen, Philemon Chelanga, Sommarat Chantarat, Michael Carter, Hassan Bashir, and Rupsha Banerjee

Financing for Development: The Global Agenda
José Antonio Ocampo

Poverty in Latin America: Feelings/Perceptions vs Material Conditions
Verónica Amarante, Maira Colacce, and Federico Scalese

Trade in Tasks: A New Perspective to International Trade, Structural Change and Economic Development
Gaaitzen J. de Vries and Marcel P. Timmer

Developmental Dilemmas: The Role of Power and Agency
William D. Ferguson

A full series listing is available at: www.cambridge.org/CEDE

For EU product safety concerns, contact us at Calle de José Abascal, 56–1°,
28003 Madrid, Spain or eugpsr@cambridge.org.

www.ingramcontent.com/pod-product-compliance
Ingram Content Group UK Ltd.
Pitfield, Milton Keynes, MK11 3LW, UK
UKHW022000030326
468620UK00021B/824